CLAUDIO FRANCO
KÁTIA TAVARES

Claudio de Paiva Franco é professor, pesquisador e autor de diversas coleções didáticas de inglês. É doutor em Estudos Linguísticos pela UFMG e mestre em Linguística Aplicada pela UFRJ. Atualmente, atua como professor e pesquisador de Língua Inglesa do Departamento de Letras Anglo-Germânicas da UFRJ. Possui certificado de proficiência em inglês pela Universidade de Cambridge. Foi professor de Educação Básica (Ensino Fundamental e Ensino Médio) e de cursos de idiomas.

Kátia Cristina do Amaral Tavares é professora, pesquisadora e autora de diversas coleções didáticas de inglês. É doutora em Linguística Aplicada e Estudos da Linguagem pela PUC-SP e mestra em Letras Anglo-Germânicas pela UFRJ. Atualmente, atua como professora e pesquisadora de Língua Inglesa do Departamento de Letras Anglo-Germânicas da UFRJ. Possui certificado de proficiência em inglês pela Universidade de Oxford. Foi professora de Educação Básica (Ensino Fundamental e Médio).

© 2019 – StandFor

Business and Content Director	Ricardo Tavares de Oliveira
Associate Editorial Director	Cayube Galas
Editorial Manager	Ana Carolina Costa Lopes
Editorial Coordinator	Renata Lara de Moraes
Assistant Editors	Carolina Nyerges, Myrian Kobayashi Yamamoto, Stela Danna
Editorial Assistant	Nathalia Xavier Thomaz
Contributors	Eneida Célia da Silva Gordo, Magueda Lopes Souza
Production Coordinator	Marcelo Henrique Ferreira Fontes
Proofreading and Copyediting Coordinator	Lilian Semenichin
Proofreading and Copyediting Supervisor	Beatriz Mendes Carneiro
Proofreaders	Amanda Lenharo, Claudia Yumiko, Lucia Passafaro, Marcella Arruda
Art Manager	Ricardo Borges
Art Coordinator	Daniela Máximo
Design	Apis Design Integrado
Cover Design	Apis Design Integrado
Art Supervisor	Patrícia De Michelis
Art Editor	Lidiani Minoda
Layout	Aero Estúdio
Digital Image Processing Technicians	Ana Isabela Pithan Maraschin, Eziquiel Racheti, Guilherme Nahes
Illustrations and Cartography Coordinator	Marcia Berne
Illustrations	Allan Arello, Andres Ramos, Arthur Mask, Bruno Ferreira, Eduardo Francisco, Galvão Bertazzi, Marcio Freitas, Tiago Holsi
Photo Researcher Supervisor	Elaine Cristina Bueno
Photo Researchers	Alessandra Pereira, Amanda Loos Von Losimfeldt, Cristiano Ribeiro, Erika Nascimento
Text Analists	Amanda Fernandes, Luiz Fernando Botter
Backup Supervisor	Silvia Regina E. Almeida
Operations Director and Print Production Manager	Reginaldo Soares Damasceno

All rights reserved. No part of this publication may be reproduced, stored in a retrieval system, or transmitted, in any form or by any means, electronic, mechanical, photocopying, recording, or otherwise, without the prior written permission of StandFor. This book is sold subject to the condition that it shall not, by way of trade or otherwise, be lent, resold, hired out, or otherwise circulated without the publisher's prior consent in any form of binding or cover than that in which it is, published and without a similar condition being imposed on the subsequent purchaser.
Whilst every effort has been made to check that the websites referred to in *English Play* were current at the time of going to press, StandFor disclaims responsibility for their content and/or possible changes. While every effort has been made to trace all the copyright holders, if any have been inadvertently overlooked, the publisher will be pleased to make the necessary arrangements at the first opportunity. Some names and identifying details have been changed to protect the privacy of individuals. The publisher would like to thank the following for permission to reproduce the photographs:

p.10: S-F/Shutterstock.com; Piotr Wawrzyniuk/Shutterstock.com; p.11: The Red Hat of Pat Ferrick; p.12: The History Of English/www.thehistoryofenglish.com; p.13: Photoroyalty/Shutterstock.com; p.14: Viktoria Yams/Shutterstock.com; p.15: © 2019 Maria Scrivan Dist.By Tribune Content Agency,LLC.; Viktoria Yams/Shutterstock.com; p.16: © The GFCE; p.17: Rawpixel.com/Shutterstock.com; p.18: La1n/Shutterstock.com; p.19: Larry Lambert / www.cartoonstock.com; M-SUR/Shutterstock.com; p. 20: www.stopthinkconnect.org; p. 21: Inspiring/Shutterstock.com; p. 23: Chris Wildt /www.CartoonStock.com; Monkey Business Images/Shutterstock.com; p. 24: paulaphoto/Shutterstock.com; Roman Samborskyi/Shutterstock.com; Ollyy/Shutterstock.com; nakaridore/Shutterstock.com; WAYHOME studio/Shutterstock.com; Ollyy/Shutterstock.com; p. 25: Ollyy/Shutterstock.com; Ollyy/Shutterstock.com; paulaphoto/Shutterstock.com; Roman Samborskyi/Shutterstock.com; WAYHOME studio/Shutterstock.com; p. 26: Africa Studio/Shutterstock.com; mmzgombic/Shutterstock.com; Ben Schonewille/Shutterstock.com; p. 27: MidoSemsem/Shutterstock.com; p. 28: pixelrain/Shutterstock.com; p. 30: Adisorn Saovadee/Shutterstock.com; adoc-photos/Corbis/Getty Images; p. 31: Rawpixel.com/Shutterstock.com; p. 33: Veley, Bradford/www.CartoonStock.com; p. 36: imtmphoto/Shutterstock.com; p. 37: Oleksandr Osipov/Shutterstock.com; p. 38: Max Mumby/Indigo/Getty Images; Theo Wargo/WireImage/Getty Images; Mike Marsland/WireImage/Getty Images; Aurelien Meunier/PSG/Getty Images; p. 40: frantic00/Shutterstock.com; Halfpoint/Shutterstock.com; Nestor Rizhniak/Shutterstock.com; Andrey_Popov/Shutterstock.com; p. 42: balabolka/Shutterstock.com; p. 44: Penguin Random house Company ; p. 45: corbac40/Shutterstock.com; p. 46: Tong Wu/TNS/Newscom/Fotoarena; p. 49: Gruhn, Mike/www.CartoonStock.com; p.50: fizkes/Shutterstock.com; p. 52: Editora Simon Pulse; p. 53: Pond's Memories/Shutterstock.com; p. 54: NeonShot/Shutterstock.com; Garfield, Jim Davis © 2019 Paws, Inc. All Rights Reserved / Dist. by Andrews McMeel Syndication; p. 55: Bonitas/Shutterstock.com; p. 56: Caroline Holden/www.CartoonStock.com; p. 57: Editora Houghton Mifflin Harcourt; © 2014 by xkcd Inc.; © 2014 by xkcd Inc.; p. 59: Garfield, Jim Davis © 2003 Paws, Inc. All Rights Reserved / Dist. by Andrews McMeel Syndication; p. 63: FloridaStock/Shutterstock.com; p. 64: EVELSON DE FREITAS/ESTADÃO CONTEÚDO; Luis Cleber/AE/AE; p. 66: John Lund/The Image Bank/Getty Images; Africa Studio/Shutterstock.com; Solarisys/Shutterstock.com; Kath Watson/Shutterstock.com; p. 68: www.dailymail.co.uk; p. 69: zizi_mentos/Shutterstock.com; p. 71: Cienpies Design/Shutterstock.com; p. 72: Lewis Team ;p. 75: Sluka, Gatis /www.CartoonStock.com; p. 76: Rawpixel.com/Shutterstock.com; p. 78: wavebreakmedia/Shutterstock.com; p. 80: Frank & Ernest, Bob Thaves © 2018 Thaves/Dist. By Andrews McMeel Syndication; p. 82: Boyko.Pictures/Shutterstock.com; N.Savranska/Shutterstock.com; p. 85: Luann, Greg Evans; p. 88: Monster Ztudio/Shutterstock.com; p. 89: Igor Levin/Shutterstock.com; p.90: Drawlab19/Shutterstock.com; Boyko.Pictures/Shutterstock.com; p. 92: photodonato/Shutterstock.com; p. 93: pinktree/Shutterstock.com; p. 94: John Keeble/Getty Images; p. 95: luma_art/Shutterstock.com; p. 97: More-Love.org; p. 98: © headspace National Youth Mental Health Foundation Ltd 2019.; p. 99: Kathy Hutchins/Shutterstock.com; Mascha Tace/Shutterstock.com; p. 101: Guisewhite, Cathy/www.CartoonStock.com; p. 102: Cris Faga/NurPhoto/Getty Images; p. 103: milanzeremski/Shutterstock.com; cifotart/Shutterstock.com; Rawpixel.com/Shutterstock.com; Sorbis/Shutterstock.com; SEE_JAY/Shutterstock.com; Volodymyr Goinyk/Shutterstock.com; Alf Ribeiro/Shutterstock.com; BestPhotoPlus/Shutterstock.com; p. 104: WWWoronin/Shutterstock.com; p. 105: GoodStudio/Shutterstock.com; p. 107: joom seeda/Shutterstock.com; p. 108: LightField Studios/Shutterstock.com; p. 111: Adbusters Media Foundation; p. 114: Dean Drobot/Shutterstock.com; p. 115: pathdoc/Shutterstock.com; p. 116: NPO/Organisation: Love Authentic; p. 118: Yiorgos GR/Shutterstock.com; p. 119: CartoonStock; p. 120: milo827/Shutterstock.com; Garfield, Jim Davis © 2011 Paws, Inc. All Rights Reserved /Dist. by Andrews McMeel Syndication.; p. 121: Garfield, Jim Davis © 2015 Paws, Inc. All Rights Reserved /Dist. by Andrews McMeel Syndication; Mascha Tace/Shutterstock.com; p.127: g-stockstudio/Shutterstock.com; Rawpixel.com/Shutterstock.com; Syda Productions/Shutterstock.com; ESB Professiona/Shutterstock.com; mimagephotography/Shutterstock.com; Zephyr_p/Shutterstock.com; Kudryashova Vera/Shutterstock.com; p. 128 Kleber Cordeiro/Shutterstock.com; p. 129: Syda Productions/Shutterstock.com; sirtravelalot/Shutterstock.com; LeManna/Shutterstock.com; p. 130: Anatoliy Karlyuk/Shutterstock.com; Icatnews/Shutterstock.com; p. 131: nasirkhan/Shutterstock.com; Mega Pixel/Shutterstock.com; p.132: Dmytro Zinkevych/Shutterstock.com; p. 133: Gorodenkoff/Shutterstock.com; studiostoks/Shutterstock.com; p. 134: GoodStudio/Shutterstock.com; p. 151: Rommel Canlas/Shutterstock.com; Teeradej/Shutterstock.com; lieber/Shutterstock.com; SpeedKingz/Shutterstock.com; Sergey Uryadnikov/Shutterstock.com; Weerachai Khamfu/Shutterstock.com; Maxim Matsevich/Shutterstock.com; Cookie Studio/Shutterstock.com; Beyla Balla/Shutterstock.com; All Stock Photos/Shutterstock.com; kelenka/Shutterstock.com; JONGSUK/Shutterstock.com;

The credits that are not mentioned here have been printed on the page where the artwork appeared due to contract demands.
Reprodução proibida: Art. 184 do Código Penal e Lei 9.610 de 19 de fevereiro de 1998.

Dados Internacionais de Catalogação na Publicação (CIP)
(Câmara Brasileira do Livro, SP, Brasil)

Franco, Claudio de Paiva
English play 9 / Claudio de Paiva Franco, Kátia Cristina Tavares do Amaral. -- 1. ed. -- São Paulo : FTD, 2019.

ISBN: 978-85-96-02492-1 (aluno)
ISBN: 978-85-96-02493-8 (professor)

1. Inglês (Ensino fundamental) I. Amaral, Kátia Cristina Tavares do. II. Título.

19-27154   CDD-372.652

Índice para catálogo sistemático:
1. Inglês : Ensino fundamental   372.652
Maria Alice Ferreira - Bibliotecária - CRB-8/7964

A - 573.637/19

1 2 3 4 5 6 7 8 9
Rua Rui Barbosa, 156 – Bela Vista, São Paulo, SP, Brasil.
CEP 01326-010 – Phone 0800 772 2300
Caixa Postal 65149 – CEP da caixa postal 01390-970
contato@standfor.com.br
www.standfor.com.br

Produção gráfica

Avenida Antônio Bardella, 300 - 07220-020 GUARULHOS (SP)
Fone: (11) 3545-8600 e Fax: (11) 2412-5375

A comunicação impressa e o papel têm uma ótima história ambiental para contar

www.twosides.org.br

Apresentação

Hey, there!

Você sabe que o inglês faz parte do seu dia a dia, certo? Ele está presente em *games* que você joga, em músicas que você ouve, em *websites* que você acessa e, possivelmente, até mesmo em etiquetas das roupas que você usa. Além disso, a língua inglesa é amplamente utilizada na comunicação entre pessoas de diferentes nacionalidades, seja presencialmente, seja *on-line*. Aprender inglês, portanto, é importante para ter acesso a tudo isso e poder participar ativamente de interações nesse idioma.

A coleção *English Play* foi preparada para que você possa desenvolver sua capacidade de utilizar a língua inglesa em diversos contextos e situações, seja para ler, ouvir, falar ou escrever em inglês. Além disso, você pode conhecer aspectos da cultura de países de língua inglesa e da diversidade linguística.

Ao longo da obra, você explora vários gêneros textuais escritos e orais e temas relevantes para você e a sociedade. Você participa de diversos tipos de atividades e descobre novas formas de pensar, sentir e agir no mundo. Para tornar tudo ainda mais desafiador e divertido, incluímos alguns "ingredientes" de *games*. Assim, ao aprender a língua inglesa, você joga, brinca, representa, ou seja, *you play*.

Como sabemos que seu papel é fundamental no processo de aprendizagem, convidamos você a se engajar nesse processo, junto com seus colegas e professor(a), de forma colaborativa, prazerosa e enriquecedora. *Let's play and learn!*

Claudio e Kátia

Contents

Conheça seu livro	6

UNIT 0 — Welcome UNIT — 8
The history of the English language 8

UNIT 1 — Staying safe online — 14
Getting Started 15
  Internet slang
Reading Comprehension .. 16
Language in Use 18
  Review: Word formation (prefixes and suffixes)
Oral Skills 20
Writing 22
  Campaign posters
English *4 Life* 23

UNIT 2 — Emotions — 24
Getting Started 25
  Describing emotions
Reading Comprehension .. 26
Language in Use 28
  Linking words/phrases
Oral Skills 30
Writing 32
  Poems
English *4 Life* 33

Play 'n' Learn 1 — 34
Games 34
Test (Units 1 and 2) 36
Project 38
My Achievements 39

UNIT 3 — The world of science — 40
Getting Started 41
  Collocations
Reading Comprehension .. 42
Language in Use 44
  Linking words/phrases
  First conditional
Oral Skills 46
Writing 48
  Science experiments
English *4 Life* 49

UNIT 4 — What if? — 50
Getting Started 51
  Collocations with *time*
Reading Comprehension .. 52
Language in Use 54
  Second conditional
Oral Skills 56
Writing 58
  Cartoons
English *4 Life* 59

Play 'n' Learn 2 — 60

- Games 60
- Test (Units 3 and 4) 62
- Project 64
- My Achievements 65

UNIT 5 Fact or fake? — 66

- Getting Started 67
  - Word groups
- Reading Comprehension .. 68
- Language in Use 70
  - Modal verbs: may/might
- Oral Skills 72
- Writing 74
  - Mind maps
- English *4 Life* 75

UNIT 6 Be a volunteer! — 76

- Getting Started 77
  - Word groups
- Reading Comprehension .. 78
- Language in Use 80
  - Modal verbs: should/must/have to
- Oral Skills 82
- Writing 84
  - Infographics
- English *4 Life* 85

Play 'n' Learn 3 — 86

- Games 86
- Test (Units 5 and 6) 88
- Project 90
- My Achievements 91

UNIT 7 Advertising and body image — 92

- Getting Started 93
  - Health problems
- Reading Comprehension .. 94
- Language in Use 96
  - Present perfect (regular verbs)
- Oral Skills 98
- Writing 100
  - Advertising posters
- English *4 Life* 101

UNIT 8 Rethinking consumerism — 102

- Getting Started 103
  - Places in town
- Reading Comprehension 104
- Language in Use 106
  - Present perfect (regular and irregular verbs)
- Oral Skills 108
- Writing 110
  - Quizzes
- English *4 Life* 111

Play 'n' Learn 4 — 112

- Games 112
- Test (Units 7 and 8) 114
- Project 116
- My Achievements 117

Language Reference — 118
Workbook — 127
Glossary — 135
Stickers — 145

Conheça seu Livro

Answer the following questions and get to know your book. Based on your total score, you can get a sticker.

1 Which unit is about volunteering?

2 And which unit is about shopping?

3 What is the main theme of **Unit 3**?

4 Which section is about the origins of the English language?

5 Which unit offers a review of word formation (prefixes and suffixes), which you studied in the previous book (8º ano)?

6 In which unit are you going to learn to describe emotions?

7 On what page does the **Workbook** start?

8 Which page offers a list of popular chat abbreviations (Internet slang)?

9 What are you going to learn in the section **English 4 Life** of the last unit?

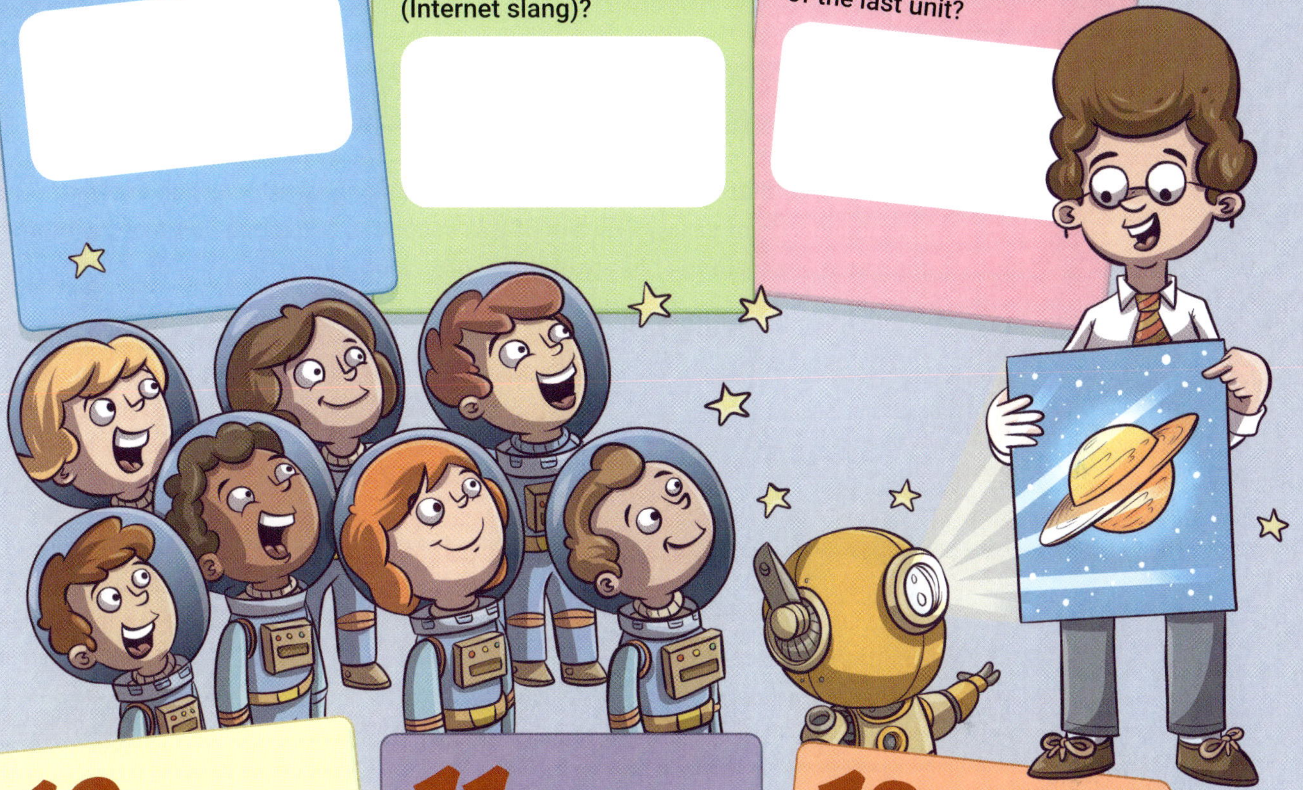

10 How many tests are there in the book?

11 What is the name of the box that comes with a QR code ()?

12 On page 144 there's an illustration for you to customize with stickers. What does it show?

Based on your total score, see what sticker you get:
- **up to 4** = a bronze medal
- **5 to 8** = a silver medal
- **9 to 12** = a golden medal

Find your sticker in the **Stickers section** and place it here.

Total: /12

Welcome Unit

The history of the English language

Did you know that what we know as the English language today has evolved over thousands of years? The aim of this section is to explore some of the most important events in the history of the English language.

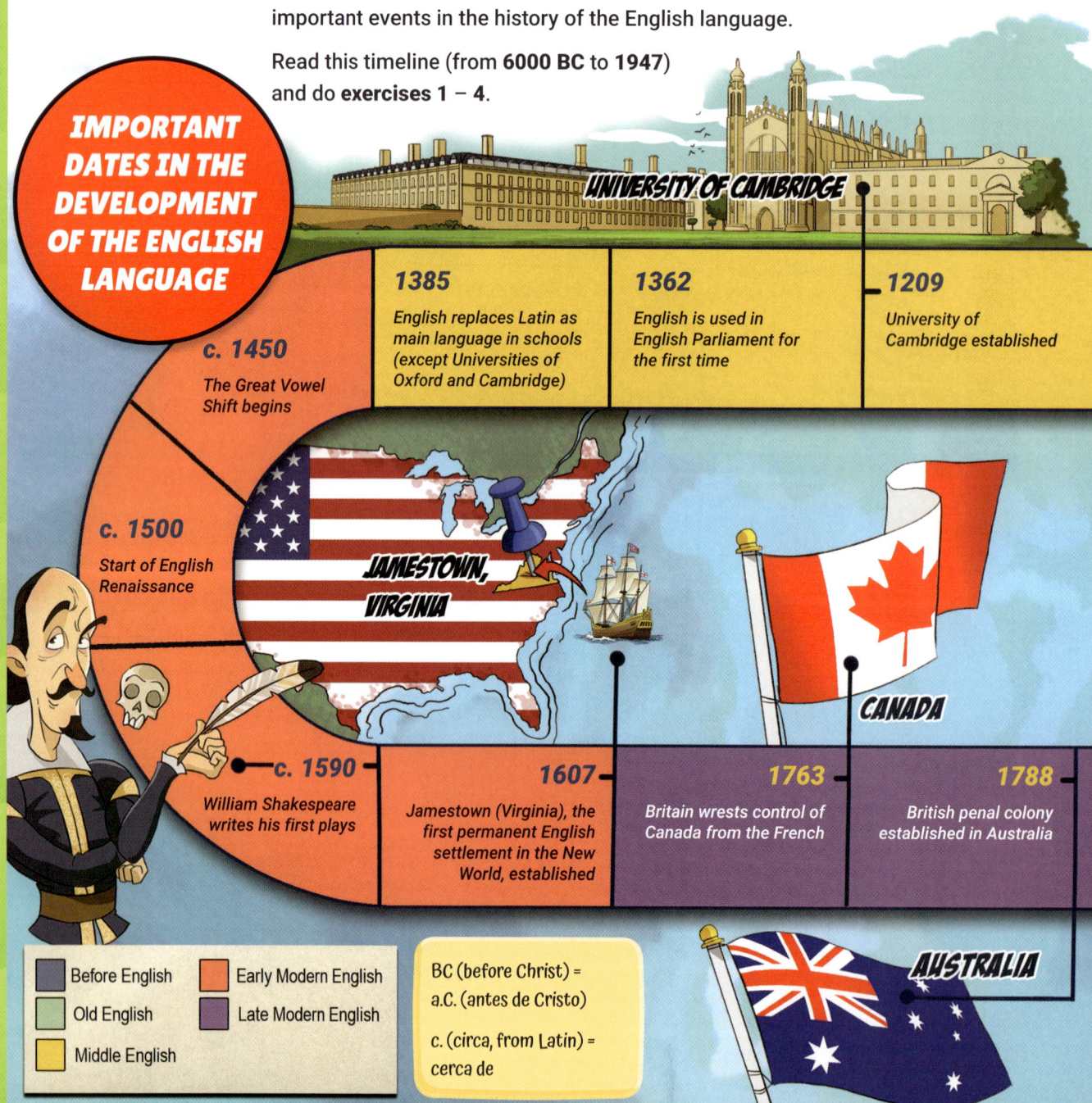

Read this timeline (from **6000 BC** to **1947**) and do **exercises 1 – 4**.

IMPORTANT DATES IN THE DEVELOPMENT OF THE ENGLISH LANGUAGE

1209 — University of Cambridge established

1362 — English is used in English Parliament for the first time

1385 — English replaces Latin as main language in schools (except Universities of Oxford and Cambridge)

c. 1450 — The Great Vowel Shift begins

c. 1500 — Start of English Renaissance

c. 1590 — William Shakespeare writes his first plays

1607 — Jamestown (Virginia), the first permanent English settlement in the New World, established

1763 — Britain wrests control of Canada from the French

1788 — British penal colony established in Australia

- Before English
- Old English
- Middle English
- Early Modern English
- Late Modern English

BC (before Christ) = a.C. (antes de Cristo)

c. (circa, from Latin) = cerca de

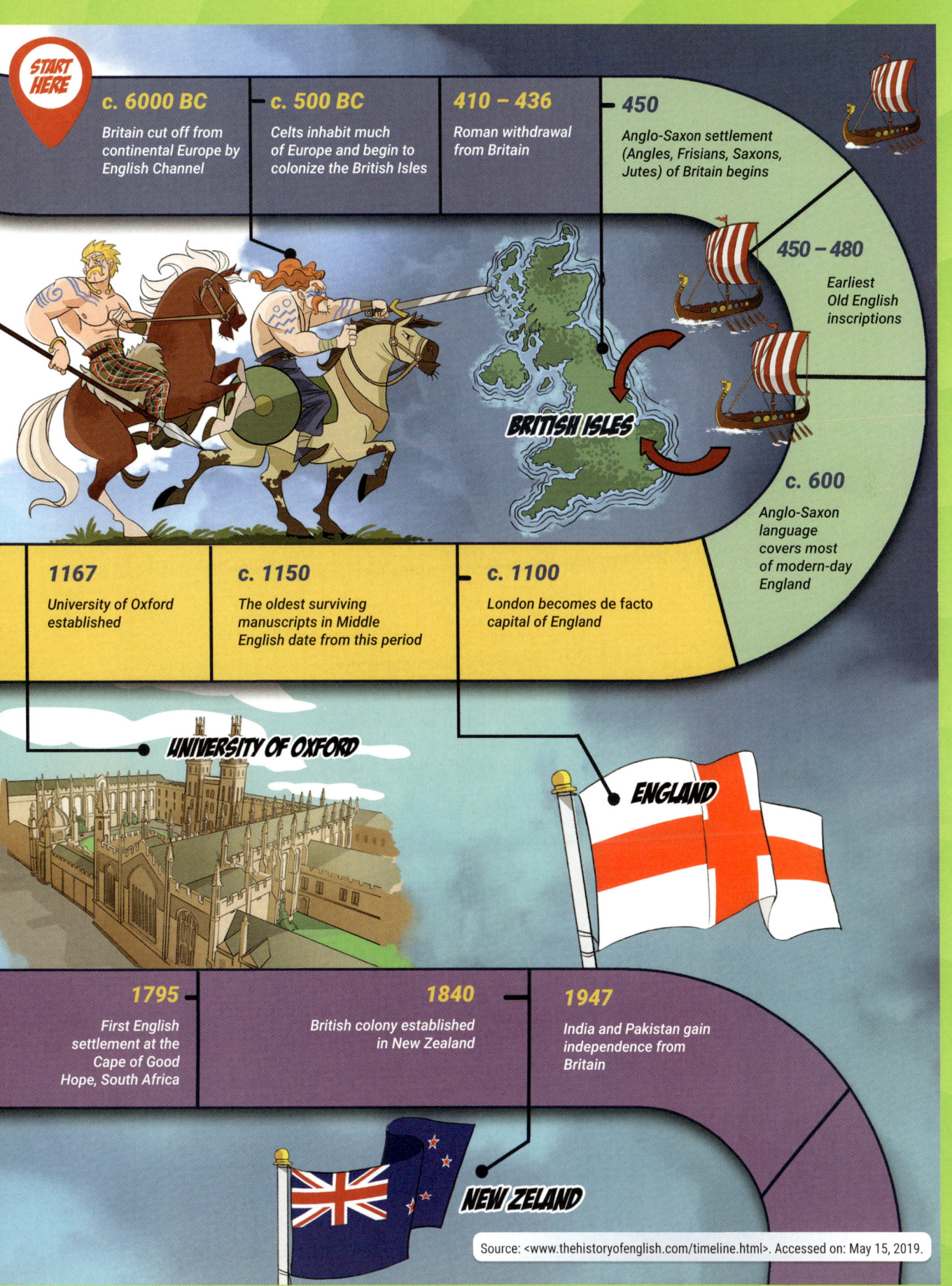

1. Answer the questions below.

   a. Which group started the colonization of the British Isles?
   _____

   b. Which four tribes arrived in Britain?
   _____

   c. When did London obtain the status of *de facto* capital of England?
   _____

2. Write **T** (True) or **F** (False). Then, correct the false statements.

   a. ◯ The University of Oxford is the oldest university in the English-speaking world.
   _____

   b. ◯ In 1385, English replaces Latin as main language in the Universities of Oxford and Cambridge.
   _____

   c. ◯ William Shakespeare writes his first plays during the stage of Middle English.
   _____

   d. ◯ India and Pakistan gain independence from Britain in 1947.
   _____

▶ On the Web

The Difference between the United Kingdom, Great Britain and England:

◂ http://livro.pro/e6udjc ▸

(Acesso em: 15 maio 2019).

University of Oxford

University of Cambridge

3. The British Empire was established by England between the late 16th and early 18th centuries. The map on the next page shows the areas of the world that were part of the British Empire. Based on the timeline on pages 8 and 9, complete the sentences about some of these areas. Then, talk to a classmate about the areas in the map that you did not know were British colonies.

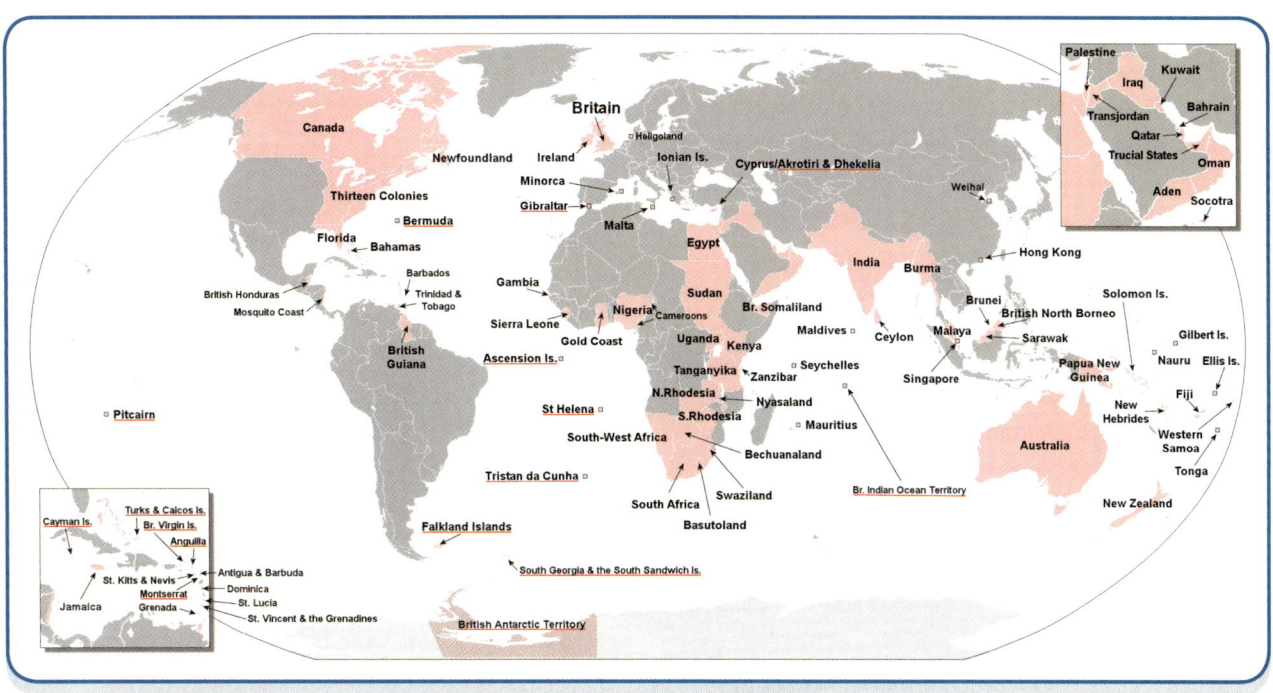

a. _____, founded in 1607, was England's first permanent settlement in the Americas.

b. After signing the Treaty of Paris in 1763, Britain gained much of France's possessions in North America, including _____.

c. A British penal colony, i.e. a settlement used to exile prisoners and separate them from the general population, was established in _____ in 1788.

d. The United Kingdom invaded and occupied the _____ in 1795. It remained a colony until it was incorporated into the independent Union of South Africa in 1910.

e. After signing the Treaty of Waitangi in 1840, a British colony was established in _____.

4 Which important event marks the change from Middle English to Early Modern English? Based on the timeline on pages 8 and 9, complete the text below.

_____ was a major change in the pronunciation of the English language. It was presumably the most significant sound change in the history of the English language. It started approximately in the 14th century and persisted into the 16th century. During that period most of the English vowels shifted their pronunciation.

Step 1: **i** and **u** drop and become **əɪ** and **əʊ**
Step 2: **e** and **o** move up, becoming **i** and **u**
Step 3: **a** moves forward to **æ**
Step 4: **ɛ** becomes **e**, **ɔ** becomes **o**
Step 5: **æ** moves up to **ɛ**
Step 6: **e** moves up to **i**
  A new **e** was created in Step 4; now that **e** moves up to **i**
Step 7: **ɛ** moves up to **e**.
  The new **ɛ** created in Step 5 now moves up.
Step 8: **əɪ** and **əʊ** drop to **aɪ** and **aʊ**

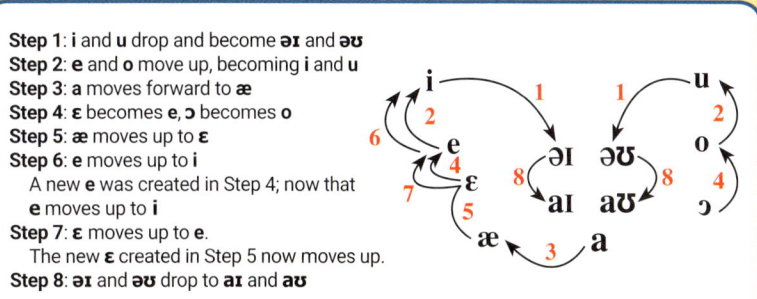

From: <https://zentrum.virtuos.uni-osnabrueck.de/wikifarm/fields/english-language/field.php/EarlyModernEnglish/GreatVowelShift>.
Accessed on: May 15, 2019.

Finding credible sources of information on the Internet can be really challenging. Below, you can see an example of a webpage about the history of the English language that offers a wide range of sources and links to other websites. Take a quick look at it and do **exercises 5** and **6**.

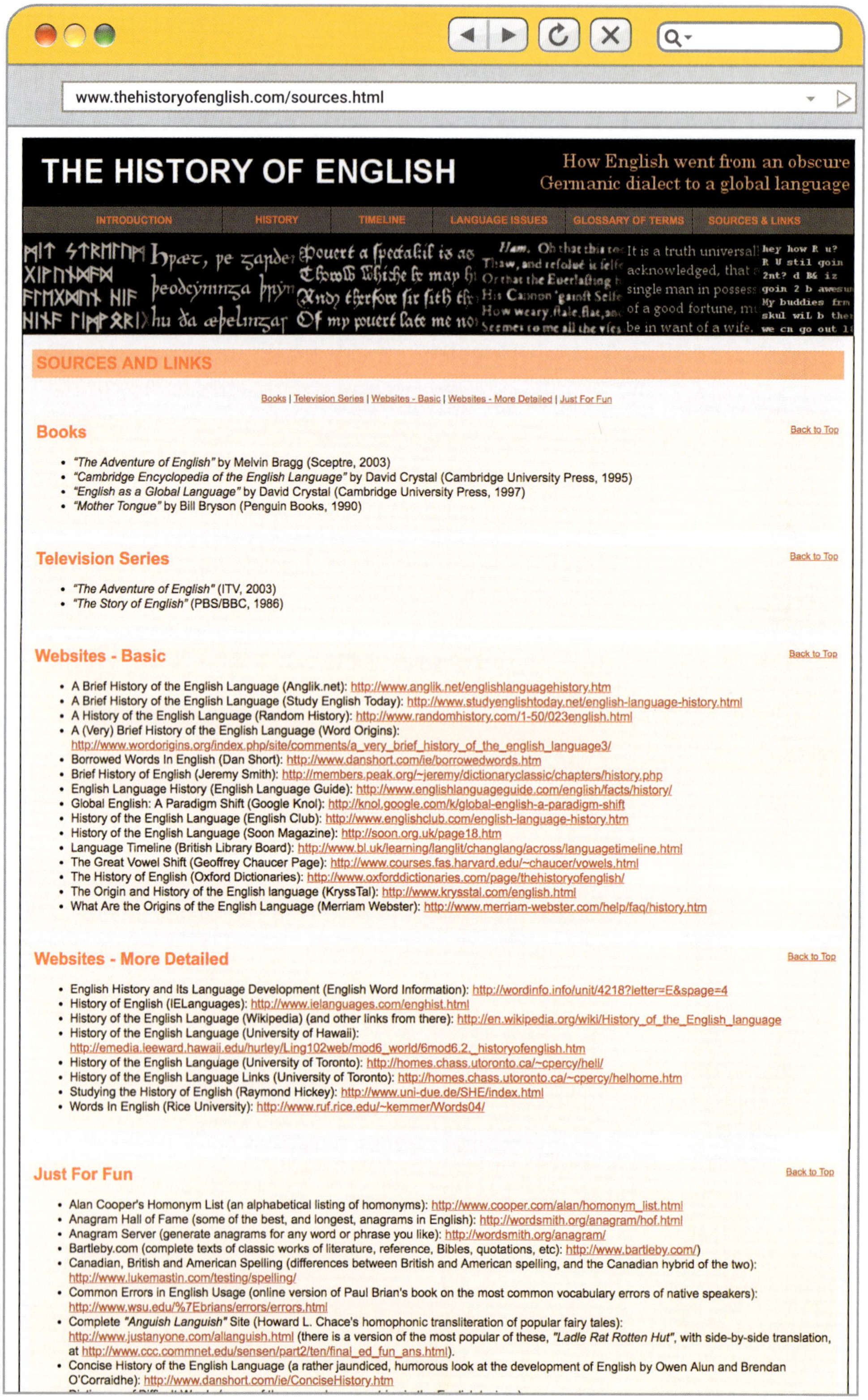

www.thehistoryofenglish.com/sources.html

THE HISTORY OF ENGLISH
How English went from an obscure Germanic dialect to a global language

INTRODUCTION | HISTORY | TIMELINE | LANGUAGE ISSUES | GLOSSARY OF TERMS | SOURCES & LINKS

SOURCES AND LINKS

Books | Television Series | Websites - Basic | Websites - More Detailed | Just For Fun

Books
Back to Top
- *"The Adventure of English"* by Melvin Bragg (Sceptre, 2003)
- *"Cambridge Encyclopedia of the English Language"* by David Crystal (Cambridge University Press, 1995)
- *"English as a Global Language"* by David Crystal (Cambridge University Press, 1997)
- *"Mother Tongue"* by Bill Bryson (Penguin Books, 1990)

Television Series
Back to Top
- *"The Adventure of English"* (ITV, 2003)
- *"The Story of English"* (PBS/BBC, 1986)

Websites - Basic
Back to Top
- A Brief History of the English Language (Anglik.net): http://www.anglik.net/englishlanguagehistory.htm
- A Brief History of the English Language (Study English Today): http://www.studyenglishtoday.net/english-language-history.html
- A History of the English Language (Random History): http://www.randomhistory.com/1-50/023english.html
- A (Very) Brief History of the English Language (Word Origins): http://www.wordorigins.org/index.php/site/comments/a_very_brief_history_of_the_english_language3/
- Borrowed Words In English (Dan Short): http://www.danshort.com/ie/borrowedwords.htm
- Brief History of English (Jeremy Smith): http://members.peak.org/~jeremy/dictionaryclassic/chapters/history.php
- English Language History (English Language Guide): http://www.englishlanguageguide.com/english/facts/history/
- Global English: A Paradigm Shift (Google Knol): http://knol.google.com/k/global-english-a-paradigm-shift
- History of the English Language (English Club): http://www.englishclub.com/english-language-history.htm
- History of the English Language (Soon Magazine): http://soon.org.uk/page18.htm
- Language Timeline (British Library Board): http://www.bl.uk/learning/langlit/changlang/across/languagetimeline.html
- The Great Vowel Shift (Geoffrey Chaucer Page): http://www.courses.fas.harvard.edu/~chaucer/vowels.html
- The History of English (Oxford Dictionaries): http://www.oxforddictionaries.com/page/thehistoryofenglish/
- The Origin and History of the English language (KryssTal): http://www.krysstal.com/english.html
- What Are the Origins of the English Language (Merriam Webster): http://www.merriam-webster.com/help/faq/history.htm

Websites - More Detailed
Back to Top
- English History and Its Language Development (English Word Information): http://wordinfo.info/unit/4218?letter=E&spage=4
- History of English (IELanguages): http://www.ielanguages.com/enghist.html
- History of the English Language (Wikipedia) (and other links from there): http://en.wikipedia.org/wiki/History_of_the_English_language
- History of the English Language (University of Hawaii): http://emedia.leeward.hawaii.edu/hurley/Ling102web/mod6_world/6mod6.2_historyofenglish.htm
- History of the English Language (University of Toronto): http://homes.chass.utoronto.ca/~cpercy/hell/
- History of the English Language Links (University of Toronto): http://homes.chass.utoronto.ca/~cpercy/helhome.htm
- Studying the History of English (Raymond Hickey): http://www.uni-due.de/SHE/index.html
- Words In English (Rice University): http://www.ruf.rice.edu/~kemmer/Words04/

Just For Fun
Back to Top
- Alan Cooper's Homonym List (an alphabetical listing of homonyms): http://www.cooper.com/alan/homonym_list.html
- Anagram Hall of Fame (some of the best, and longest, anagrams in English): http://wordsmith.org/anagram/hof.html
- Anagram Server (generate anagrams for any word or phrase you like): http://wordsmith.org/anagram/
- Bartleby.com (complete texts of classic works of literature, reference, Bibles, quotations, etc): http://www.bartleby.com/
- Canadian, British and American Spelling (differences between British and American spelling, and the Canadian hybrid of the two): http://www.lukemastin.com/testing/spelling/
- Common Errors in English Usage (online version of Paul Brian's book on the most common vocabulary errors of native speakers): http://www.wsu.edu/%7Ebrians/errors/errors.html
- Complete *"Anguish Languish"* Site (Howard L. Chace's homophonic transliteration of popular fairy tales): http://www.justanyone.com/allanguish.html (there is a version of the most popular of these, *"Ladle Rat Rotten Hut"*, with side-by-side translation, at http://www.ccc.commnet.edu/sensen/part2/ten/final_ed_fun_ans.html).
- Concise History of the English Language (a rather jaundiced, humorous look at the development of English by Owen Alun and Brendan O'Corraidhe): http://www.danshort.com/ie/ConciseHistory.htm

On the Web

The History of English – Sources and Links:

◂ http://livro.pro/edeexn ▸

(Acesso em: 15 maio 2019).

5 Based on the websites listed in the category "Websites – Basic", write down the ones that refer to the items below.

   a. This website offers an interactive timeline that allows you to explore the evolution of English language and literature.

   _____

   b. These two webpages, which can be found in the online version of two respected English dictionaries, refer to the origins of the English language.

   _____
   _____

6 Use the checklist below to evaluate the websites listed in the category "Websites – Basic". After evaluating them, which ones would you recommend?

   _____
   _____

	YES	NO
1. Is the author listed on the website and can you contact him/her for clarification?*		
2. Is the author an expert or a respected person in his/her field?		
3. Are the sources of information stated?		
4. Does the website contain links for further information?		
5. Are all the links working?		
6. Has the website been recently updated?*		
7. Does the title of the page tell you what it is about?		
8. Does the website present facts?		
9. Is the website free of errors in grammar and spelling?		
10. Are there images of good quality?		

*Check the header and the footer of the website for author information and last update.

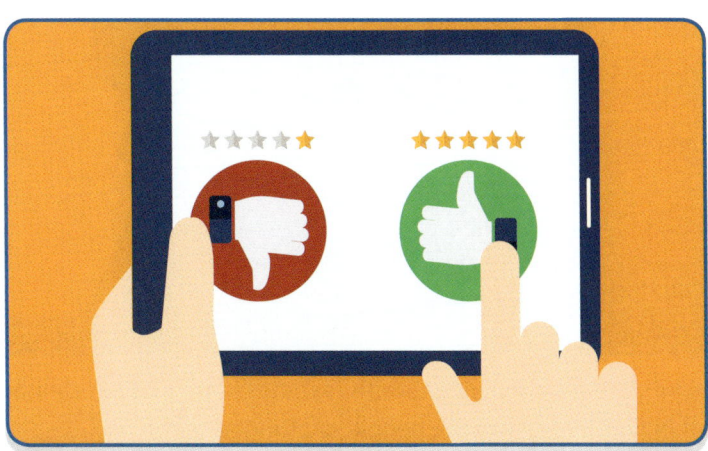

UNIT 1
Staying safe online

Learning Objectives

- to talk about Internet safety;
- to learn vocabulary related to Internet slang;
- to review **word formation (prefixes and suffixes)**;
- to explore **campaign posters**.

The picture shows a smartphone with text messages. Which elements are used in this chat? What are the people chatting about?

Getting Started

Internet slang

1 What do this cartoon and the picture on page 14 have in common?

_____
_____
_____
_____
_____
_____

2 How often do you use emojis/emoticons? Which ones are your favorites?

_____

3 Chat abbreviations are also very popular when it comes to communicating on the Internet. Match the columns below and find out what some of them are.

a. 4 — thanks
b. BRB — face to face
c. BTW — I don't know
d. F2F — hugs and kisses
e. FYI — short for "for"
f. IDK — be right back
g. ILY — for your information
h. LOL — by the way
i. THX/THNX — I love you
j. XOXOXO — laughing out loud

4 Do you know any other chat abbreviations? If so, which one(s)?

_____

Challenge!

Which abbreviations/onomatopoeia in Portuguese are equivalent to LOL?

Extra Challenge!

DIY and ASAP are two very popular abbreviations. What do they mean?

 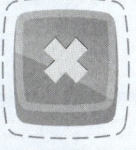

▶ **On the Web**

List of Chat Abbreviations

◀ http://livro.pro/9apfhk ▶

(Acesso em: 5 maio 2019).

Reading Comprehension

Pre-Reading

1 Read the campaign poster on the right, which is related to the text you are going to read in **exercise 3**. What is it about? In your opinion, what do you need to take into consideration when surfing the web?

_____
_____
_____

2 Before reading the following text, focus on its **title** and **source**. What do you expect to read about?

_____

Reading

3 Read the text below to check your predictions.

Privacy Tips for Teens

You learn, connect with friends and play games online. Just as you look both ways before crossing the street (which we hope you do), be sure you are using the Internet safely and securely. The first step is to STOP. THINK. CONNECT.: take safety measures, think about the consequences of your actions and connect knowing you are protecting yourself from an unhappy surprise.

Share With Care

- **What you post can last a lifetime:** Before posting online, think about what others might learn about you and who might see it in the future — teachers, parents, colleges and potential employers. Share the best of yourself online.

- **Be aware of what's being shared:** Be aware that when you post a picture or video online, you may also be sharing information about others or personal details about yourself like where you live, go to school or hang out.

[...]

Personal Information Is Like Money. Value It. Protect It.

- **Know what's being collected, who is collecting it and how it will be used:** Information about you, such as the games you like to play, what you search for online and where you shop and live, has value just like money. Be thoughtful about who gets that information and how it's collected through apps and websites. [...]

From: <https://staysafeonline.org/wp-content/uploads/2017/09/STOP.-THINK.-CONNECT.-Privacy-Tips-for-Teens.pdf>. Accessed on: May 5, 2019.

> aware = atento(a), ciente

4 Answer each question with a fragment from the text.

a. What do teens usually use the Internet for?
_____
_____

b. How long can a post last?
_____
_____

c. What does the author compare personal information online to?
_____
_____

5 Read the fragment below, focus on the word **like** and mark the correct statements about it.

"Personal Information Is **Like** Money."

a. ◯ **Like** is a verb.

b. ◯ **Like** is a linking word.

c. ◯ **Like** is used to make a comparison.

d. ◯ **Like** is used to introduce an example.

e. ◯ The fragment is equivalent to "Personal information **likes** money."

6 Now read these fragments, focus on the words in **bold** and mark the correct statement about them.

I. "[...] personal details about yourself **like** where you live, go to school or hang out."

II. "Information about you, **such as** the games you like to play, what you search for online and where you shop and live [...]"

a. ◯ **Like** and **such as** are used to make comparisons.

b. ◯ **Like** and **such as** are used to introduce examples.

Post-Reading

7 Discuss the questions below with your classmates.

a. In your opinion, are the tips given in the text useful for teens? Do you put them into practice?

b. What other safety measures do you usually take in order to stay safe online?

> **▶ On the Web**
>
> Tips for Safe Web Surfing
>
> ◄ http://livro.pro/ccycxh ►
>
> (Acesso em: 5 maio 2019).

Challenge!

Write down three other words that end in **-tion**.

Extra Challenge!

Write down three other words that end in **-al**.

Language in Use

Review: Word formation (prefixes and suffixes)

Read the fragments from the text on page 16 and do **exercises 1** and **2**.

I. "[...] be sure you are using the Internet **safely** and **securely**."

II. "[...] connect knowing you are protecting yourself from an **unhappy** surprise."

III. "Be **thoughtful** about who gets that information [...]"

1 Match the columns.

a. -ly as in *safely, securely* means ◯ "not"

b. un- as in *unhappy* means ◯ "full of"

c. -ful as in *thoughtful* means ◯ "in a particular way"

2 Complete each statement with the correct word in parentheses.

a. un- is an example of a _____. (prefix/suffix)

b. -ful is used to form _____. (adjectives/adverbs)

c. -ly is used to form _____. (adjectives/adverbs)

3 Now read this fragment from the text on page 16 and mark the correct alternatives.

"[...] you may also be sharing **information** about others or **personal** details about yourself [...]"

a. The suffix -tion turns *verbs* into

◯ nouns. ◯ adjectives.

b. The suffix -al can turn various words, often *nouns*, into

◯ adverbs. ◯ adjectives.

4 Complete these Internet safety tips. Use the words in parentheses and an appropriate **suffix**.

a. Never share personal information, such as passwords and your _____. (locate)

b. Think _____ before posting pictures or videos of yourself. (careful)

c. _____ check your privacy settings on social media. (regular)

d. Make sure your Internet _____ is secure. (connect)

Read this cartoon and do **exercises 5** and **6**.

"These symbols are indecipherable. I think these must be the precursors of CAPTCHAS."

CAPTCHA (Completely Automated Public Turing test to tell Computers and Humans Apart) = teste de Turing público completamente automatizado para diferenciação entre computadores e humanos

5 What do the characters think about the symbols?

a. ◯ They are easy to read and understand.

b. ◯ They are impossible to read or understand.

6 The word **indecipherable** contains a prefix (**in-**) and a suffix (**-able**). Based on the cartoon, what do they mean?

a. ◯ In- means "inside" and -able means "like".

b. ◯ In- means "not" and -able means "able to".

7 Complete the text with the correct words in parentheses.

Some content on the Internet may be illegal, _____ (safe/unsafe), _____ (offensive/inoffensive) or _____ (suitable/unsuitable) for some age groups. _____ (Appropriate/Inappropriate) content may include: violence, pornography, extremist and criminal behavior. Therefore, it is extremely relevant that children develop digital literacy skills and learn how to report online content that makes them feel _____ (comfortable/uncomfortable).

Language Note

illegal = *not* legal
irrelevant = *not* relevant

Go to **Language Reference** on **page 118**.

 **Oral Skills**

1 Read two campaign posters about Internet safety and discuss the questions below with your classmates. Use the expressions from the box to help you.

From: <www.stopthinkconnect.org/resources/preview/different-password-poster>. Accessed on: May 5, 2019.

From: <www.stopthinkconnect.org/resources/preview/wifi-hotspots-poster>. Accessed on: May 5, 2019.

a. How do these campaign posters try to catch the reader's attention?

b. Do you think they are effective pieces of advertising? Why (not)?

c. Do you put the tips given in the posters into practice? Why (not)?

d. What steps do you usually follow to stay safe online?

e. In your opinion, is the Internet safe for young people? Why (not)?

f. Do your parents monitor Internet use at home? If so, how? What do you think about it?

> **Expressing an opinion:** I think/believe (that)...; In my opinion/view...
> **Asking for an opinion:** What do you think?; Do you agree (with me)?
> **Expressing agreement:** I agree with you.; (I think/believe) You're right.
> **Expressing disagreement:** I don't agree with you.; I don't think so.
> **Different ways of saying 'yes':** Yep.; Yeah.; Sure.
> **Different ways of saying 'no':** Nope.; Not really.; Not at all.

2 Listen to the recording and notice that it is about specific lessons that students from public schools in the USA are taking. What are the lessons about?

_____

3 Listen to the recording again and complete the chart with information about the school mentioned in it.

Name of the school:	
Located in:	, USA
Estimated number of students:	

Pronunciation Note

In spoken English, it is very common to use *hundreds* instead of *thousands* when saying large numbers. For example, 1,500 can be described as *fifteen hundred*, instead of *one thousand five hundred* (or *one and a half thousand*).

4 Listen to the recording once more and take notes on its main ideas. Then, use your notes to help you mark the correct answers.

a. What do almost all of the students from the school mentioned have in common?

○ They use social networking sites to communicate.

○ They are victims of cyberbullying.

b. What are the three recommendations that these students receive?

○ "Be nice online."

○ "Don't talk to strangers."

○ "Always change your passwords."

○ "Don't share personal information."

○ "Don't agree to meet people who approach you on the Web."

c. What is said about Virginia?

○ It is the state in the USA with the highest number of public schools.

○ It is the first state in the USA to require Internet safety lessons in school.

5 Listen to the recording another time and check your answers.

 # Writing

In this unit you have read different campaign posters about Internet safety on pages 16 and 20. They are persuasive campaign posters that encourage teens to stay safe online. Visit <www.stopthinkconnect.org/resources> (under "Posters") to find other examples of campaign posters related to the topic.

- Based on the campaign posters you have read in this unit, write your own campaign poster about Internet safety in order to share tips for teens. Your text should be directed toward young people.

Follow these instructions to write your text.

1. Think of an Internet safety tip that can be useful for teens.
2. Look for potential images and choose a memorable one that relates to the topic of the text.
3. Define your slogan or catchy phrase. Then, write a draft of the text.
4. Place the slogan/catchy phrase, text and images in a visually attractive configuration. Keep your poster visual.
5. Exchange campaign posters with a classmate and discuss them. Take into consideration the following:
    a. Is the campaign poster suitable for the target audience?
    b. Do the pictures make the text more attractive?
    c. Does the slogan/catchy phrase express the main idea of the text?
6. Make the necessary corrections.
7. Create the final version of your campaign poster. You can use a computer to design it.

It is time to share your campaign poster with your classmates and other people. You can also publish it on the school's website/blog or on a non-profit organization's website. Based on people's reactions to your text, you can continue to improve it.

ENGLISH 4 LIFE

Read this cartoon and do **exercises 1 - 3**.

"Mom's always telling me to look both ways, don't talk to strangers, and change my passwords."

1 What Internet security tip does the boy's mom always give him?

_____

2 What can we infer from the cartoon? Mark the correct alternatives.

a. ◯ The boy is talking to his mother.

b. ◯ Surfing the web is part of the boy's routine.

c. ◯ The boy's mother worries about Internet safety.

3 Why is the present continuous ("Mom's always telling me…") used in the cartoon?

a. ◯ To talk about actions happening at the moment of speaking.

b. ◯ To talk about fixed plans in the near future.

c. ◯ To talk about repeated actions.

4 Mark the sentences below that use the present continuous for the same reason as the cartoon.

a. ◯ The students are surfing the Internet.

b. ◯ She's always sending boring videos to us.

c. ◯ They are opening a new website next month.

d. ◯ You're constantly forgetting your passwords.

Language Note

"My mom's always telling me…" = *My mom always tells me…*

The present continuous with words like "always", "forever", "constantly" expresses an irritating habit to the speaker. Notice that the meaning is the same as in the present simple, but with a negative idea.

Unit 1 23

UNIT 2 Emotions

Learning Objectives
- to talk about emotions;
- to learn adjectives that describe emotions;
- to use linking words/phrases;
- to explore poems.

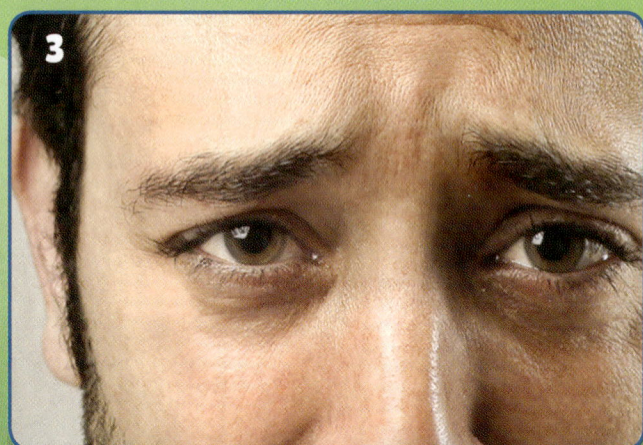

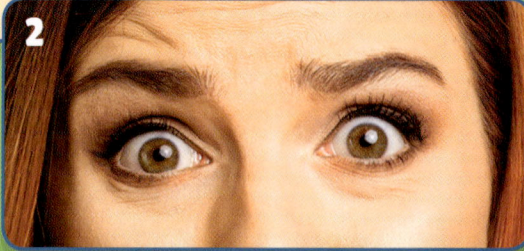

In your opinion, is it possible to identify a person's emotion by looking only at the eyes? Why (not)? Do your emotions show on your face easily?

Getting Started

Describing emotions

1 Look at the photos on page 24 again and mark the adjective that best describes how each person is feeling.

a. Photo 1 ◯ angry ◯ focused
b. Photo 2 ◯ calm ◯ worried
c. Photo 3 ◯ sad ◯ surprised
d. Photo 4 ◯ frustrated ◯ joyful
e. Photo 5 ◯ anxious ◯ serious
f. Photo 6 ◯ bored ◯ excited

Pronunciation Note

③ The suffix **-ous** is pronounced as /əs/. Listen to adjectives that end in **-ous** and notice how they are pronounced. Then, listen and repeat.

anxious • dangerous • famous • furious • nervous • ridiculous • serious

2 Listen to the recording and repeat the adjectives in **exercise 1**.

3 Match the photos on page 24 with the faces below. Write **1-6**. Then, review your answers to **exercise 1** and make changes if necessary.

a. Photo ◯   b. Photo ◯   c. Photo ◯

d. Photo ◯   e. Photo ◯   f. Photo ◯

4 The adjectives in the box can also describe the emotions of the people in **exercise 3**. In pairs, ask and answer how they are feeling as in the example.

> annoyed • concerned • excited • focused • ~~furious~~ • unhappy

Student A: How is the woman in photo 1 feeling?
Student B: She's feeling furious.

5 Listen to the recording and repeat the adjectives in **exercise 4**.

Challenge!

Name three other adjectives that describe **positive emotions**.

Extra Challenge!

Name three other adjectives that describe **negative emotions**.

 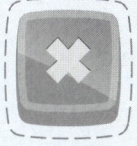

Reading Comprehension

Pre-Reading

1 Before reading the text, focus on its **title**, **structure** and **source**. Then, mark the correct answers.

   a. What is the target audience of the text?

     ◇ People in general.   ◇ Doctors and health professionals.

   b. Which organ of the human body is the text about?

  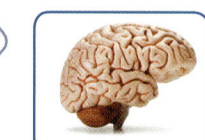 

2 What do you expect to read in the text below?

_____

_____

Reading

3 Read the text below to check your predictions.

▶ **On the Web**

Reading People

◀ http://livro.pro/oxehpe ▶

(Acesso em: 5 maio 2019).

The emotional brain

There's *motion* inside the word *emotion*, and for good reason. Emotions not only bring on highs and lows but also communicate via gesture and expression. These physical manifestations provide the crucial distinction separating emotion from other behaviors. Emotions manifest themselves outwardly in visible changes to the body, such as muscle contractions, blood vessel dilations, and facial expressions. Powerful emotions can deeply carve events into memory, alter behavior and physical health, contribute to good (or bad) decision making, and even cause a person to be literally scared to death. Scientists are only beginning to understand their importance.

Aristotle classified more than a dozen emotions, including envy and pity. Today, most scientists recognize fear, anger, sadness, and joy, while some add surprise and disgust, referring to the complete list of six as "primary" or "universal" emotions. Many casual observers would add love to the list, but researchers are divided over classifying it as emotion or drive.

From: NATIONAL GEOGRAPHIC. *Your Brain Revised & Updated*: A User's Guide – 100 Things You Never Knew. Jan. 5, 2018. p. 91.

4 According to the text, how much do scientists know about emotions?

a. ◯ They know everything about how the brain processes emotions.

b. ◯ They are just starting to understand the importance of emotions.

5 Answer the questions below.

a. What provides an important distinction between emotion and other behaviors?

_____

b. Which six emotions are scientifically recognized today as universal emotions?

_____

6 Write **T** (True) or **F** (False). Then, correct the false statements.

a. ◯ Muscle contractions and facial expressions are two examples of visible changes to the body when emotions manifest themselves.

_____
_____

b. ◯ Powerful emotions cannot be responsible for changing a person's behavior.

_____
_____

c. ◯ Aristotle only classified two emotions – envy and pity.

_____
_____

d. ◯ Not all researchers believe love is an emotion.

_____
_____

Aristotle

7 In "researchers are divided over classifying it as emotion or drive", what does **drive** mean?

a. ◯ A strong natural need or desire.

b. ◯ Determination and energy to succeed.

Post-Reading

8 Discuss the questions below with your classmates.

a. In your opinion, can powerful emotions modify behavior and physical health? Can you give examples to support your answer?

b. Do you think love is an emotion? Why (not)?

Unit 2 **27**

Language in Use

Linking words/phrases

Read the fragments from the text on page 26 and do **exercises 1** and **2**.

I. "Emotions **not only** bring on highs and lows **but also** communicate […]"

II. "[…] visible changes to the body, **such as** muscle contractions, blood vessel dilations, and facial expressions."

III. "Many casual observers would add love to the list, **but** researchers […]"

IV. "Today, most scientists recognize fear, anger, sadness, and joy, **while** some add surprise and disgust […]"

1 Complete the statements with **I**, **II**, **III** or **IV**.

a. In fragments _____ and _____, you can find *linking words* in bold.

b. In fragments _____ and _____ you can find *linking phrases* in bold.

2 What idea do the linking words/phrases in **bold** express? Complete the table with **addition**, **contrast** or **exemplification**.

a. _____	such as like	for example for instance
b. _____	but however	while whereas
c. _____	not only… but (also) in addition	besides moreover

Language Note

Linking words (*and*, *like*, *but*, etc.) and **linking phrases** (*for example*, *in addition to*, *as a result*, etc.) can be used to join two or more words, sentences or clauses. They are used to show relationships between ideas (e.g. addition, contrast, exemplification, result, etc.).

3 Rewrite the sentences with the linking words/phrases given as in the example.

a. We can send emotional messages through different mechanisms, like facial expressions and posture.
SUCH AS: *We can send emotional messages through different mechanisms, such as facial expressions and posture.*

b. It's easier to fake positive body language, whereas negative body language is more difficult.
WHILE: _____

c. It's not difficult to predict what can annoy people. For instance, showing up an hour late will almost always annoy the average person.
FOR EXAMPLE: _____

Read this poem and do **exercises 4** and **5**.

Feelings

Feelings go up and feelings go down
There are feelings inside us all spinning around.
Sometimes they're good and sometimes they're bad
But feelings are something that everyone has.
Being shut out and feeling unsafe are feelings that
I think that
Everyone
Hates.

By Natalie

From: <www.cyh.com/HealthTopics/HealthTopicDetailsKids.aspx?p=335&np=287&id=1530>. Accessed on: May 5, 2019.

4 Which part of the poem refers to the fact that feelings change?

_____

5 Rewrite the first line of the poem ("Feelings go up and feelings go down") with the linking phrase **not only... but also**. _____

Read this text, focus on the linking words in **bold** and do **exercises 6** and **7**.

Relationships

Like emotions, everyone has some sort of relationship with other people. **Unless** you are a castaway on an island, you interact with people everyday. Relationships with parents, friends, and significant others (**like** a boyfriend or girlfriend) can be rewarding and **also** frustrating.

From: <www.pamf.org/teen/life/>. Accessed on: May 5, 2019.

castaway = náufrago

6 Mark the correct statements.

a. ◯ **Like** in "Like emotions" is used to make a comparison.

b. ◯ **Unless** expresses contrast.

c. ◯ **Like** in "like a boyfriend or girlfriend" is used to introduce examples.

d. ◯ **Also** expresses addition.

7 Mark the sentence below that is equivalent in meaning to "Unless you are a castaway on an island, you interact with people everyday."

a. ◯ **If** you are a castaway on an island, you interact with people every day.

b. ◯ **Except if** you are a castaway on an island, you interact with people every day.

Language Note

The linking word **if** expresses a *condition*.

Go to **Language Reference** on **page 118**.

Unit 2

Oral Skills

1 What makes you feel happy? And angry?

2 Listen to the beginning of a talk recorded by educator Sophie Zadeh. Mark the question that is answered by her in the talk.

a. ◯ How can we measure happiness?

b. ◯ How many types of feelings are there?

c. ◯ Are there universal expressions of emotion?

3 Listen to the recording again and mark the correct answers.

a. How many muscles in the human face can be activated to create different expressions?

◯ About thirty.   ◯ About forty.

b. What did Charles Darwin theorize about?

◯ That emotional expression was a common human feature.

◯ That emotions were learned behaviors that varied across cultures.

c. What did theorist Silvan Tomkins claim about emotional states and their associated facial expressions?

◯ That they were universal.

◯ That they were varied across cultures.

Charles Darwin

4 Listen to the recording once more and check your answers.

5 Read two quotes about emotions and discuss the questions below with your classmates. Use the expressions from the box to help you.

> "Every day we have plenty of opportunities to get angry, stressed or offended. But what you're doing when you indulge these negative emotions is giving something outside yourself power over your happiness. You can choose to not let little things upset you." (Joel Osteen Read)

KLEIN, Allen. *Positive thoughts for troubling times*: A renew-your-spirit guide. Coral Gables: Mango Publishing, 2019.

> "How do I control my emotions? How do I stop getting angry so often, or how do I stop being sad? And I think there's a really important distinction to understand is that you can't completely control your emotions. What you control is your reaction to your own emotions. And a lot of people don't ever make that separation for what goes on with them." (Mark Manson)

From: <www.businessinsider.com/how-to-control-your-emotions-2017-12>. Accessed on: May 5, 2019.

Expressing an opinion:
I think/believe (that)...;
In my opinion/view...

Asking for an opinion:
What do you think?; Do you agree (with me)?

Expressing agreement:
I agree with you.;
I think/believe you're right.

Expressing disagreement:
I don't agree with you.;
I don't think so.

Different ways of saying 'yes':
Yep.; Yeah.; Sure.

Different ways of saying 'no':
Nope.; Not really.; Not at all.

a. Do you agree with Joel Osteen Read? Why (not)?

b. How do you usually deal with negative emotions?

c. In your opinion, can we control our emotions? Why (not)?

d. Do you agree with Mark Manson? Why (not)?

e. How often do you talk about your feelings? Who do you usually talk to?

▶ **On the Web**

Emotions
◀ http://livro.pro/vqr8d9 ▶
(Acesso em: 5 maio 2019).

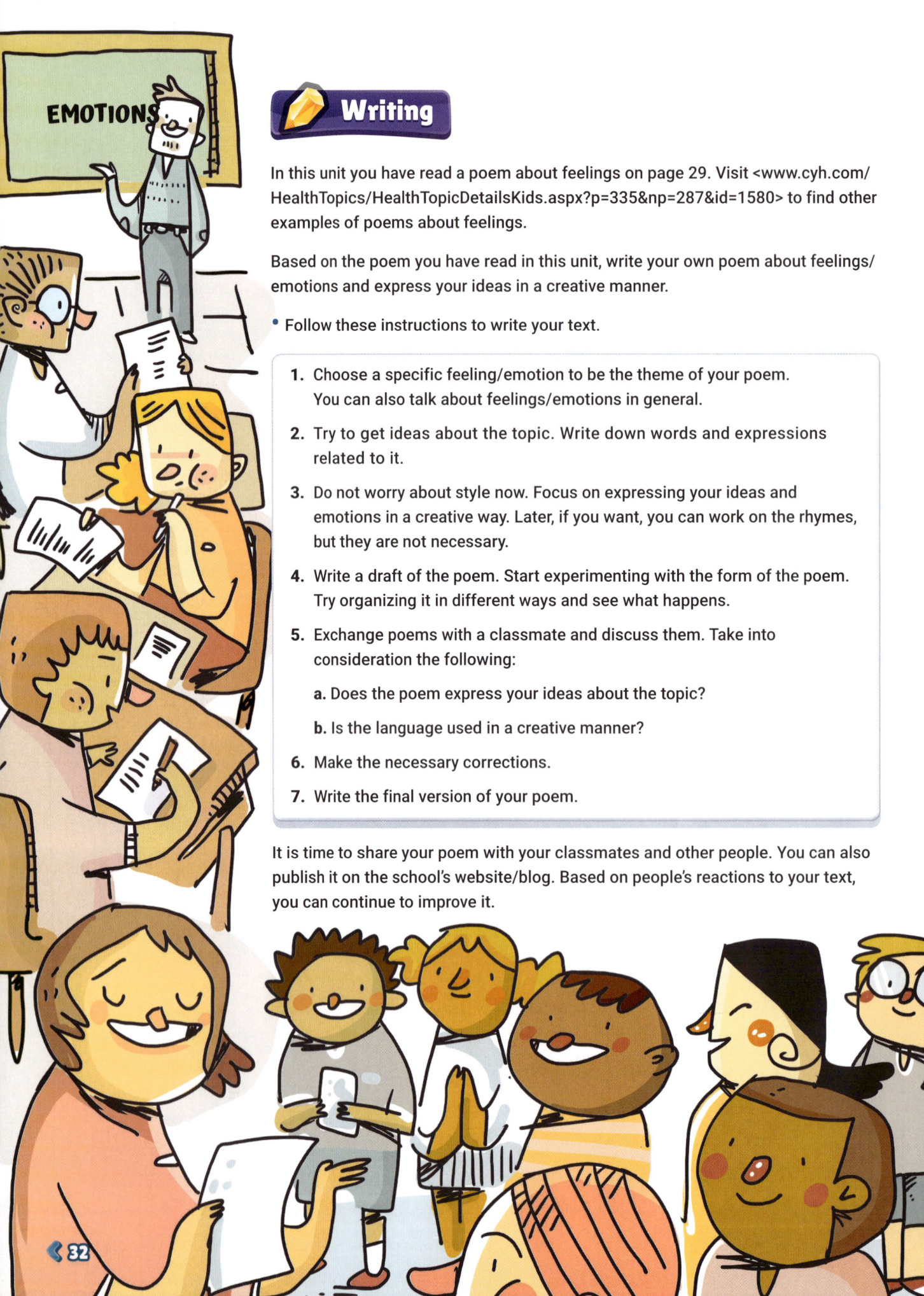

Writing

In this unit you have read a poem about feelings on page 29. Visit <www.cyh.com/HealthTopics/HealthTopicDetailsKids.aspx?p=335&np=287&id=1580> to find other examples of poems about feelings.

Based on the poem you have read in this unit, write your own poem about feelings/emotions and express your ideas in a creative manner.

• Follow these instructions to write your text.

1. Choose a specific feeling/emotion to be the theme of your poem. You can also talk about feelings/emotions in general.

2. Try to get ideas about the topic. Write down words and expressions related to it.

3. Do not worry about style now. Focus on expressing your ideas and emotions in a creative way. Later, if you want, you can work on the rhymes, but they are not necessary.

4. Write a draft of the poem. Start experimenting with the form of the poem. Try organizing it in different ways and see what happens.

5. Exchange poems with a classmate and discuss them. Take into consideration the following:

    a. Does the poem express your ideas about the topic?

    b. Is the language used in a creative manner?

6. Make the necessary corrections.

7. Write the final version of your poem.

It is time to share your poem with your classmates and other people. You can also publish it on the school's website/blog. Based on people's reactions to your text, you can continue to improve it.

ENGLISH 4 LIFE

Read this cartoon and do **exercises** 1 and 2.

"Gee, Bill, you're not still upset about that e-mail I sent you yesterday, are you?"

Language Note

The interjection **Gee** is very common in American English and it is often used to show that you are surprised, impressed or annoyed.

1 Based on Bill's emoticon face, how is he feeling?

a. ◯ Upset.   b. ◯ Excited.   c. ◯ Surprised.

2 Based on the facial expression of Bill's workmate and the use of the interjection **Gee**, how is he feeling?

a. ◯ Angry.   b. ◯ Surprised.   c. ◯ Excited.

3 Focus on the interjections in **bold** and infer how people are feeling. Match the columns.

a. We won the game. **Yay**!   ◯ surprised

b. **Ugh**, I'm not gonna eat that!   ◯ excited

c. **Wow**! What a fantastic house.   ◯ sorry

d. I'm so glad everything went well. **Phew**!   ◯ disgusted

e. **Oops**! I forgot your name again. ◯ relieved

Pronunciation Note

7 Listen to the interjections below and repeat them.

a. gee /dʒiː/   b. oops /ʊps/   c. phew /fjuː/   d. ugh /ʌg/   e. yay /jeɪ/   f. wow /waʊ/

Challenge!

In "Ouch! That hurt!", what does **ouch** express?

Extra Challenge!

In "Yummy! I love chocolate cake!", what does **yummy** express?

Unit 2

Play 'n' Learn 1

 **Games**

It's time to play a prefix game in groups of three. Follow the instructions, play 'n' learn!

INSTRUCTIONS

1. In each turn, players have 60 seconds to write down as many words with the prefix given as possible.
2. The player with the highest number of correct words is the winner.

ROUND 1 (PREFIX: UN–)	ROUND 2 (PREFIX: IN–)	ROUND 3 (PREFIX: DIS–)

It's time to play a suffix game in groups of three. Follow the instructions, play 'n' learn!

INSTRUCTIONS

1. In each turn, players have 60 seconds to write down as many words with the suffix given as possible.
2. The player with the highest number of correct words is the winner.

ROUND 1 (SUFFIX: –TION)	ROUND 2 (SUFFIX: –FUL)	ROUND 3 (SUFFIX: –ABLE)

Play 'n' Learn 1 35

TEST (UNITS 1 AND 2)

1 What do the chat abbreviations in the box stand for? Find the appropriate words/expressions for them.

> 4 • BTW • F2F • FYI • IDK • LOL • THX/THNX • XOXOXO

a. thanks _____

b. I don't know _____

c. face to face _____

d. by the way _____

e. short for "for" _____

f. hugs and kisses _____

g. laughing out loud _____

h. for your information _____

SCORE: _____ / 16 (2 each)

2 Complete these Internet safety tips. Use the words in parentheses and an appropriate **prefix** or **suffix**.

a. Avoid public Wi-Fi. It is often _____. (secured)

b. Don't _____ click on links in emails. (automatic)

c. Use a firewall. It is an electronic barrier that blocks _____ access to your computer. (authorized)

d. Be _____ when upgrading an app as it can create additional costs. (care)

e. Choose strong passwords that are _____ difficult for cybercriminals to guess. (extreme)

SCORE: _____ / 30 (6 each)

3 Complete the text with the correct words in parentheses.

> **Tell an adult if someone makes _____ (appropriate/inappropriate) suggestions to you or makes you feel _____ (comfortable/uncomfortable) online.**

From: <www.bullying.co.uk/cyberbullying/how-to-stay-safe-online/>.
Accessed on: May 20, 2019.

SCORE: _____ / 6 (3 each)

4 Focus on the interjections in **bold** and infer how people are feeling. Match the columns.

a. **Oops**! I forgot her birthday.

b. **Ugh**, I'm not going to drink that!

c. We won the football match. **Yay**!

d. **Wow**! What a beautiful apartment.

e. I'm so glad everything went well. **Phew**!

◯ surprised
◯ excited
◯ relieved
◯ sorry
◯ disgusted

SCORE: _____/ 20 (4 each)

5 Rewrite the sentences with the linking words/phrases given.

a. People experience emotions when they are awake and also when they are dreaming.

   Not only… but also:

   _____
   _____

b. We convey emotions through different mechanisms, like facial expressions and gestures.

   Such as:

   _____
   _____

c. You can easily fake positive emotions, whereas negative emotions are very difficult to fake.

   While:

   _____
   _____

d. Different colors spark different emotions in us. For instance, blue helps to calm down a person.

   For example:

   _____
   _____

SCORE: _____/ 28 (7 each)

TOTAL: _____/ 100

Go to **My Achievements** on **page 39**.

Project

TASK

In small groups, create four memes that show famous people expressing different emotions (anger, disgust, fear, joy, sadness, surprise). You can use a meme generator (website or app) to easily add text to images. Then, gather all memes you and your classmates created to make a poster about emotions and share them among teachers, family members, friends, and other people from your community. You can also share the memes on the Internet.

▶ On the Web

Meme Generator

◀ http://livro.pro/i6pmrs ▶

(Acesso em: 15 abr. 2019).

Some examples:

W-H-Y
ARE YOU DOING THIS TO ME?

WHEN I SEE A SLICE OF PIZZA =D

WHAT?
DON'T SAY IT AGAIN!

WHAT AM I SUPPOSED TO DO?

Evaluating

Answer the questions below to evaluate the development of the project.

a. What have you learned from the project?

b. What was the group interaction like? What needs improving?

c. Would you do anything differently? If so, what? Why?

My Achievements

Go back to **Unit 1** and **Unit 2** and check how many ticks (✓) you have. Use the table below to help you count the total number of ticks.

UNIT 1	CHALLENGE!	EXTRA CHALLENGE!
page 15		
page 18		
UNIT 2	**CHALLENGE!**	**EXTRA CHALLENGE!**
page 25		
page 33		

TOTAL NUMBER OF TICKS: _____/8

Check what you get:

- **1 - 2 ticks** = 1 sticker (a video player app)
- **3 - 5 ticks** = 2 stickers (a video player app and a contacts app)
- **6 - 8 ticks** = 3 stickers (a video player app, a contacts app and an instant messenger app)

Find your stickers in the **Stickers** section and place them on page 144.

Based on your total score in **Test (Units 1 and 2)**, see what you get:

- **60 to 79** = a bronze medal sticker
- **80 to 89** = a silver medal sticker
- **90 to 100** = a golden medal sticker

Find your sticker in the **Stickers** section and place it here.

PLACE YOUR STICKER HERE.

How do you feel about your **commitment** and **participation** in classes? Consider the development of the four skills (reading, writing, listening and speaking).

Find your sticker in the **Stickers** section and place it above.

Play 'n' Learn 1

UNIT 3 The world of science

Learning Objectives

- to talk about science and experiments;
- to learn about collocations;
- to use linking words/phrases;
- to use the **first conditional**;
- to explore **science experiments**.

The photos are related to the world of science. In your opinion, how can we take advantage of science in our daily life?

Getting Started

Collocations

1. Which photo on page 40 shows a person **doing an experiment** at a physics museum? And which photo shows people trying to **find a cure** for a disease through a microscope?

2. Focus on the words in **bold** in **exercise 1** and notice that they usually go together (**do** + **experiment**, **find** + **cure**). They are examples of collocations. Complete this table with words in the box and learn new collocations.

answer • physics • research • shopping • solution • time

DO	FIND

3. Complete this flowchart with words from the box and learn new collocations.

curiosity • explanation • feedback • problems • questions

How science works

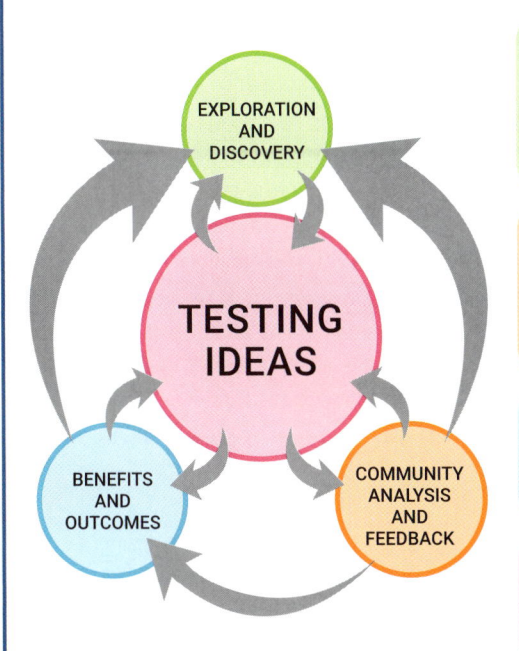

- **EXPLORATION AND DISCOVERY**
  - Reading about science discoveries
  - Making observations
  - Asking _____

- **TESTING IDEAS**

- **COMMUNITY ANALYSIS AND FEEDBACK**
  - Receiving _____
  - Discussing with classmates
  - Coming up with new questions/ideas

- **BENEFITS AND OUTCOMES**
  - Solving everyday _____
  - Satisfying _____
  - Answering questions

- Gathering data
- Coming up with an _____
- Interpreting observations

Source: <https://undsci.berkeley.edu/lessons/pdfs/complex35_flow_posterv.pdf>. Accessed on: May 10, 2019.

On the Web

English Collocations Dictionary

◂ http://livro.pro/x8jymh ▸

(Acesso em: 10 maio 2019).

Challenge!

Which multi-word verb in the flowchart means "to find or produce a question, an explanation etc."

Extra Challenge!

Which expression in the flowchart means "coletar dados" in Portuguese?

Unit 3

Pronunciation Note

When a word contains **sc + e** or **sc + i** (as in science /'saɪəns/), **sc** sounds /s/. Listen to the words below and mark the ones in which **sc** sounds /s/.

a. ◯ adole**sc**ent

b. ◯ con**sc**ious

c. ◯ di**sc**ipline

d. ◯ fa**sc**inating

e. ◯ **sc**ene

f. ◯ **sc**hool

g. ◯ **sc**ientist

h. ◯ **sc**reen

Reading Comprehension

Pre-Reading

1 Before reading the text, focus on its **title** and **subheadings**. Then, mark what you expect to read about science.

a. ◯ It is stimulating.

b. ◯ It is expensive.

c. ◯ It is useless for society at times.

d. ◯ It is a dynamic process of discovery.

Reading

2 Read the text below to check your predictions.

https://undsci.berkeley.edu/article/0_0_0/whatisscience_01

What is science?

[...]

- **Science is both a body of knowledge and a process**. In school, science may sometimes seem like a collection of isolated and static facts listed in a textbook, but that's only a small part of the story. Just as importantly, science is also a process of discovery that allows us to link isolated facts into coherent and comprehensive understandings of the natural world.

- **Science is exciting.** Science is a way of discovering what's in the universe and how those things work today, how they worked in the past, and how they are likely to work in the future. Scientists are motivated by the thrill of seeing or figuring out something that no one has before.

- **Science is useful**. The knowledge generated by science is powerful and reliable. It can be used to develop new technologies, treat diseases, and deal with many other sorts of problems.

- **Science is ongoing**. Science is continually refining and expanding our knowledge of the universe, and as it does, it leads to new questions for future investigation. Science will never be "finished."

[...]

From: <https://undsci.berkeley.edu/article/0_0_0/whatisscience_01>. Accessed on: May 10, 2019.

---

knowledge = conhecimento

thrill = animação, empolgação

▶ **On the Web**

What Is Science?

◂ http://livro.pro/f59qrf ▸

(Acesso em: 10 maio 2019).

3 Based on the text, mark the correct statements about science.

a. ◯ Science is both a body of knowledge and the process for building that knowledge.

b. ◯ Science is a way of learning about what is in the natural world.

c. ◯ Science relies on testing ideas with knowledge gathered from the natural world.

d. ◯ Science is complete. Scientific ideas are absolute and unchanging.

4 Find examples or evidence in the text that support the following ideas.

a. Science is exciting.

_____
_____

b. Science is useful.

_____
_____
_____

5 Focus on the multi-word verbs in **bold** and mark the correct answers.

a. In "figuring out something that no one has before", what does **figure out** mean?

◯ Understand something.

◯ Calculate the cost of something.

b. In "deal with many other sorts of problems.", what does **deal with** mean?

◯ Perform.

◯ Solve.

Post-Reading

6 Discuss the questions below with a classmate.

a. According to the text, "in school, science may sometimes seem like a collection of isolated and static facts listed in a textbook". In your opinion, how can science be seen in a more comprehensive way at school? In small groups, make a list of three ideas that can be put into practice at your school to broaden people's perspectives on science. Then, share your list with other classmates and get to know different viewpoints on the same topic.

broaden = ampliar, expandir

b. Do you think science can help us understand both the natural and the social world? Why or why not?

Unit 3 43

Language in Use

Linking words/phrases

1 Read this fragment from the text on page 42, focus on **like** and mark the correct statements about it.

> [...] science may sometimes seem **like** a collection of isolated and static facts [...]

dangle = balançar
propeller = hélice
repel = repelir
rub = esfregar

a. ◯ **Like** is a verb.
b. ◯ **Like** is used to make a comparison.
c. ◯ **Like** is a linking word.
d. ◯ **Like** is used to introduce an opposition.

Read the science experiment below and do **exercises** 2 and 3.

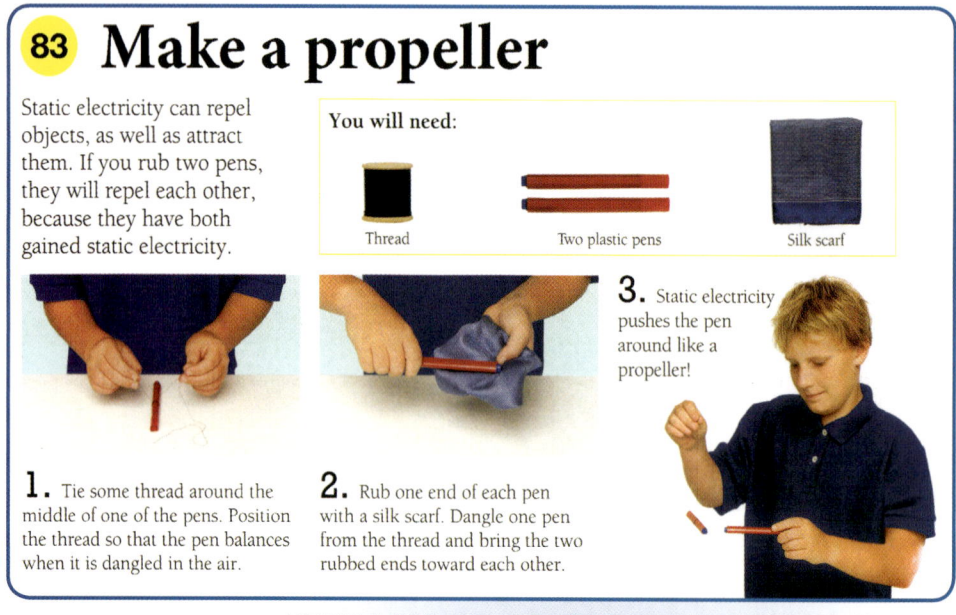

83 Make a propeller

Static electricity can repel objects, **as well as** attract them. **If** you rub two pens, they will repel each other, **because** they have both gained static electricity.

You will need:
Thread — Two plastic pens — Silk scarf

1. Tie some thread **around** the middle of one of the pens. Position the thread **so that** the pen balances **when** it is dangled in the air.

2. Rub one end of each pen **with** a silk scarf. Dangle one pen from the thread **and** bring the two rubbed ends toward each other.

3. Static electricity pushes the pen around **like** a propeller!

ARDLEY, Neil. 101 *Great Science Experiments*. New York: Dorling Kindersley, 2014. p. 97.

Attract and **repel** are two examples of true cognates in English. **Push**, on the contrary, is an example of a false cognate or "false friend" in English. It looks like *puxar* in Portuguese, but it has a different meaning (*empurrar*).

2 According to the text, what happens if you rub two pens together, after rubbing them with a piece of silk?

a. ◯ They will repel each other.
b. ◯ They will attract each other.

3 Focus on the linking words/phrases in **bold** and use them to complete the table.

MEANING	LINKING WORDS/PHRASES
addition	
cause	
comparison	

MEANING	LINKING WORDS/PHRASES
condition	
purpose	
time	

First conditional

4 Mark the sentence that is equivalent in meaning to the fragment below.

> If you rub two pens, they will repel each other […].

a. ◯ Two pens will repel each other if you rub them.

b. ◯ Two pens will rub each other if you repel them.

5 Now look at the science experiment on the right and mark the sentence that describes it correctly.

a. ◯ If you run a comb through your hair a few times, it will repel bits of paper.

b. ◯ If you run a comb through your hair a few times, it will attract bits of paper.

Based on the sentences in **exercises 4** and **5**, do **exercises 6** and **7**.

6 Mark the correct statement about those sentences.

a. ◯ They refer to situations that are **not real** or **not probable now**.

b. ◯ They refer to situations that are **real** and **possible in the future**.

▶ On the Web

Static Electricity

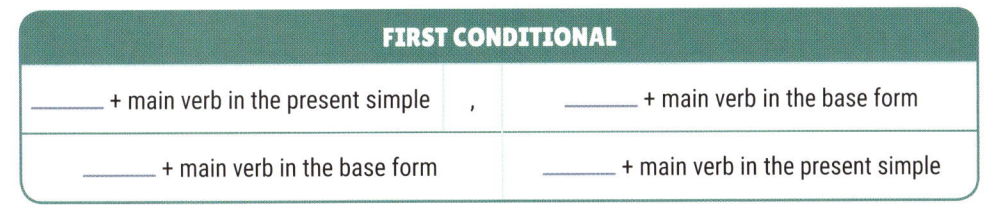

◂ http://livro.pro/yqrbqk ▸

(Acesso em: 10 maio 2019).

Simple static electricity experiment with hair comb

① ②

7 Complete this table.

FIRST CONDITIONAL	
_____ + main verb in the present simple ,	_____ + main verb in the base form
_____ + main verb in the base form	_____ + main verb in the present simple

8 Complete these quotes about science. Use the **first conditional**.

a. "Science in textbooks is not fun. But if you _____ (start) doing science yourself, you _____ (find) delight." (Masatoshi Koshiba)

From: <www.japantimes.co.jp/news/2002/11/01/national/nobel-laureates-hope-deeds-will-inspire-science-boom/#.XOVia8hKiUk>. Accessed on: May 10, 2019.

b. "There is no science in creativity. If you _____ (not give) yourself room to fail, you _____ (not innovate)." (Bob Iger)

From: <www.investors.com/news/management/leaders-and-success/bob-iger-restored-disneys-magic-kingdom-through-creative-management/>. Accessed on: May 10, 2019.

Go to **Language Reference** on page 119.

Oral Skills

1 Is there a science lab at your school? Does your school promote science fairs?

2 Before listening to part of an interview with Hannah Herbst, a 16-year-old student and scientist, read this short text and mark the correct statements about her.

About Hannah Herbst

Hannah Herbst's love for science and passion for helping others started when she was young, at a summer engineering camp. Her desire to help her nine-year-old pen pal from Africa, where many people have little or no access to electricity, led her to create an ocean energy probe prototype. The purpose of this innovation was to bring stable electricity and fresh water access to people of developing countries by using untapped energy from ocean currents.

Hannah values volunteering and, nowadays, she spends several hours working with students who want to be science fair competitors. In 2015, she was awarded the title of "America's Top Young Scientist".

Source: <www.hannahherbst.com>. Accessed on: May 10, 2019.

a. ◯ Hannah created a water-powered innovation to bring electricity to developing countries.

b. ◯ She has a pen pal living in an African developing country.

c. ◯ She was named America's Top Young Scientist in 2015.

d. ◯ She doesn't get involved in volunteering.

▶ **On the Web**

Hannah Herbst

◀ http://livro.pro/s5tr3h ▶

(Acesso em: 10 maio 2019).

3 Now listen to part of an interview with Hannah Herbst. What question does she answer?

a. ◯ "How did you get into science?"

b. ◯ "What did you invent as a scientist?"

c. ◯ "What motivates you to find solutions to problems?"

4 Listen to the recording again and take notes on its main ideas. Then, use your notes to help you complete the sentences about Hannah with expressions from the box. There are two extra expressions.

> create robots • energy poverty problem • science clubs • summer camp •
> the only girl • the only kid • theater and sports

a. Hannah was interested in _____ when she was in elementary school.

b. Before going to an engineering _____, she studied science by memorizing things from a textbook.

c. In that camp, where Hannah was _____ on the program, she learned how to innovate and _____.

d. This experience inspired her to help her pen pal's _____.

Different ways of saying 'yes':
Sure./Totally./Absolutely./You bet!/By all means.

Different ways of saying 'no':
Nope/No way./Not really./Not at all./Not in a million years.

5 Listen to the recording once more and check your answers.

6 Interview your classmates to find out about their views on science. Complete the chart below with your classmates' names when their answer is affirmative (e.g. Sure. / Absolutely.). Ask extra questions and take turns as in the example.

FIND SOMEONE WHO...	CLASSMATES' NAMES
believes electricity is the greatest discovery.	
has some experience in doing science experiments.	
thinks robots should be used in education.	
agrees that modern technology increases stress.	
is against animal cloning.	

Student A: Do you believe electricity is the greatest discovery?

Student B: Sure. And you?

Student A: Well, I think so. Thanks to electricity, we now have smartphones and computers.

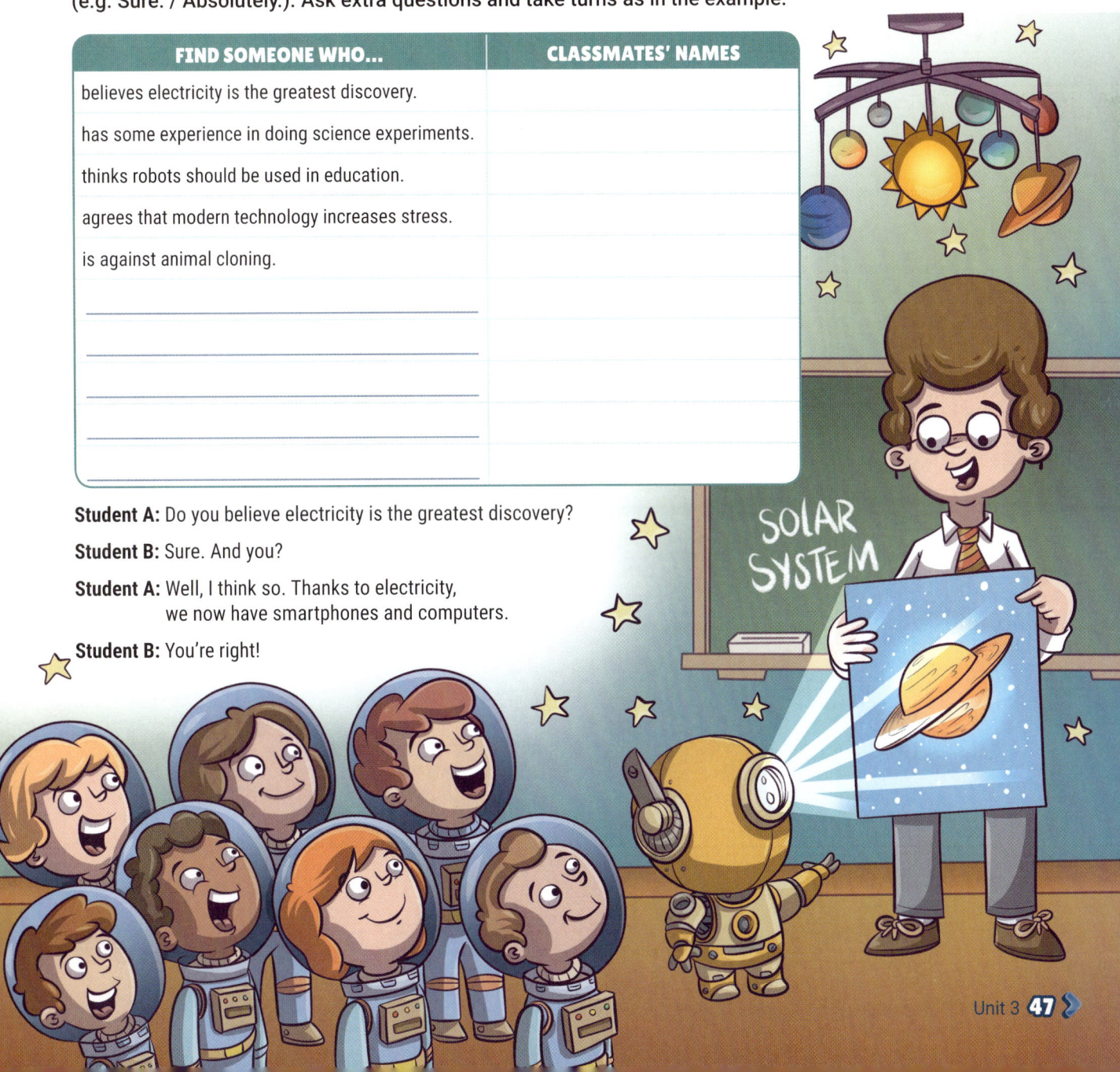

Student B: You're right!

Writing

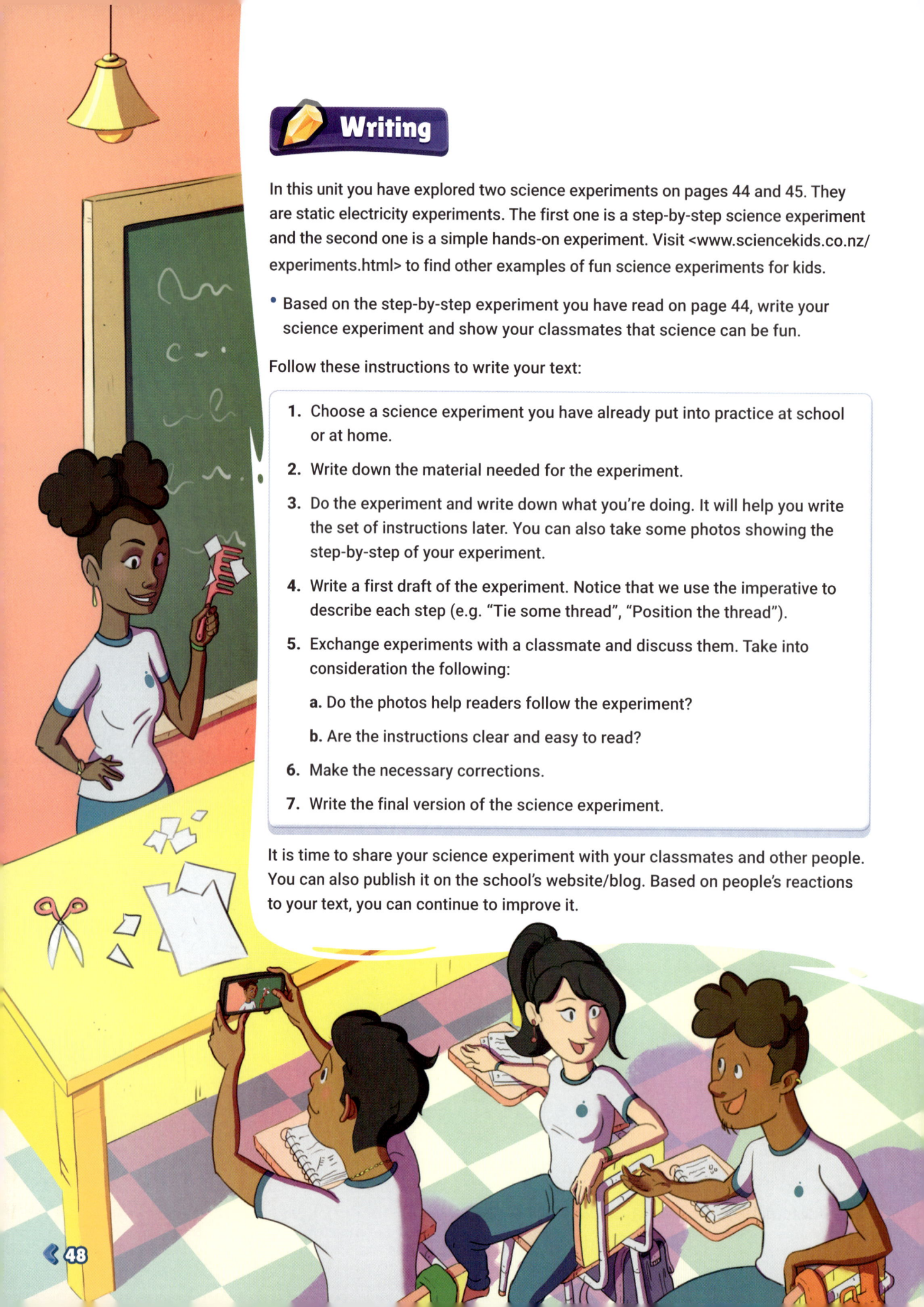

In this unit you have explored two science experiments on pages 44 and 45. They are static electricity experiments. The first one is a step-by-step science experiment and the second one is a simple hands-on experiment. Visit <www.sciencekids.co.nz/experiments.html> to find other examples of fun science experiments for kids.

- Based on the step-by-step experiment you have read on page 44, write your science experiment and show your classmates that science can be fun.

Follow these instructions to write your text:

1. Choose a science experiment you have already put into practice at school or at home.
2. Write down the material needed for the experiment.
3. Do the experiment and write down what you're doing. It will help you write the set of instructions later. You can also take some photos showing the step-by-step of your experiment.
4. Write a first draft of the experiment. Notice that we use the imperative to describe each step (e.g. "Tie some thread", "Position the thread").
5. Exchange experiments with a classmate and discuss them. Take into consideration the following:

    a. Do the photos help readers follow the experiment?

    b. Are the instructions clear and easy to read?

6. Make the necessary corrections.
7. Write the final version of the science experiment.

It is time to share your science experiment with your classmates and other people. You can also publish it on the school's website/blog. Based on people's reactions to your text, you can continue to improve it.

ENGLISH 4 LIFE

Read this cartoon and do **exercises 1** and **2**.

snowy slopes = encostas nevadas

wordplay = jogo de palavras

Language Note

bacteria (plural) / bacterium (singular)

1 The expression "hit the scopes" is a wordplay with the expression "hit the slopes", which means "go skiing". What is the visual reference to skiing in the cartoon?

a. ◯ The microscopes look like snowy slopes.

b. ◯ The bacteria are doing a science experiment.

2 Answer the questions.

a. Are the bacteria having a formal or an informal conversation? _____

b. Which word is used to refer to "microscopes"? _____

c. Which word does the character use to refer to the others? _____

3 **Dude** is an example of <u>slang</u> in English. Slang is very informal language or specific words/expressions used by a particular group of people or region. Circle the slang word used in each sentence below.

a. Hey, buddy. Could you do me a favor?

b. I just got a gig as a freelance journalist.

c. He was the best singer. He totally nailed it!

d. She's always reading those tacky romance novels.

4 For each definition below, write the appropriate slang word used in **exercise 3**.

a. a job, especially a temporary one: _____

b. of cheap quality or in bad style: _____

c. do something successfully: _____

d. friend, pal: _____

Challenge!

Write down another slang word for **dude** with an equivalent meaning.

Extra Challenge!

In "I can't listen to her love songs. They are so cheesy!", focus on the slang word **cheesy**. To which slang word in **exercise 4** is it equivalent in meaning?

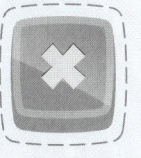

Unit 3

UNIT 4

What if?

Learning Objectives

- to talk about hypothetical situations;
- to learn about collocations with *time*;
- to use the **second conditional**;
- to explore **cartoons**.

'What if?' statements throw fuel on the fire of stress and worry. Things can go in a million different directions, and the more time you spend worrying about the possibilities, the less time you'll spend focusing on taking action that will calm you down and keep your stress under control.

(Travis Bradberry)

From: <www.brainyquote.com/quotes/travis_bradberry_734843>. Accessed on: May 10, 2019.

Do you agree with the quote by Travis Bradberry? Why (not)?

Are you the kind of person who prefers to worry about the possibilities or to focus on taking action?

Getting Started

Collocations with *time*

1 How do you manage your time? Complete the table below.

I OFTEN SPEND *MORE* TIME...	I OFTEN SPEND *LESS* TIME...
playing games	watching TV

2 Read the quote on page 50 again and notice that the words **spend** and **time** go together, which is an example of *collocation*. Complete the sentences with the expressions in the box and learn new collocations using the word *time*. Make inferences.

> free/spare time • kill time • make time • right on time • take your time • ~~tell someone the time~~ • waste time

a. Can you ____tell me the time____, please? I'm not wearing my watch.

b. Do you like listening to music in your _____?

c. I'm busy this week, but I'll try to _____ to read a novel.

d. I usually _____ on the phone while waiting for the school bus.

e. Don't _____ on video games and do your homework right away.

f. I got to school at 7 a.m. That was _____.

g. No need to hurry. _____!

> **On the Web**
>
> More Collocations Using the Word *Time*
>
> ◄ http://livro.pro/8tirnv ►
>
> (Acesso em: 10 maio 2019).

Challenge!

In "I didn't finish the test because I ran out of time.", what does **run out of time** mean?

Extra Challenge!

In "She's into video games big time.", what does **big time** mean?

Unit 4

Reading Comprehension

Pre-Reading

1 Before reading the text, focus on its **structure**, **title** and **picture**. Then, mark the correct answers.

    a. What is the target audience of the text?
        ◯ Teens.   ◯ Female activists.

    b. Where can you find the text below?
        ◯ On the cover of a teen magazine.   ◯ On the introductory chapter of a book.

2 What do you expect to read about in the text?

_____

Reading

3 Read the text below to check your predictions.

Introduction

You Can So Change the World

There's more to being a teenager than dating drama, shopping, and video games. You know this, but it probably seems like the rest of the world doesn't. There are things you care about and things that you want to change. There are things that have to change. You have the power to change them.

Right now in the United States, twenty-six percent of the population is under eighteen. That's more than seventy million people. Imagine what it would be like if you and everyone around you got to tell the world what you think. Don't wait until you're old enough to vote to take action. Starting today, starting right now, you can make your voice heard on the issues that matter to you.

This book is about activism, a word that is intimidating to a lot of people. When they hear about an "activist," they imagine some crazy guy with a picket sign on the evening news, protesting something they've never even heard about. Well, that's one kind of activist. I like to think of an activist as someone who acts on his or her beliefs and values. Acting on your beliefs can happen in a lot of ways. You might buy only organic food, or you might circulate a petition to ask for organic food in your school cafeteria. Some activists are agitators; some aren't. Some are connected to larger organizations, and others do things solo. Activism is a continuum, and you have to tailor your actions in a way that's comfortable for you. But I bet that once you get going and see the changes you can make, you'll find yourself becoming more and more outspoken and committed. […]

From: HALPIN, Mikki. *It's Your World – If You Don't Like It, Change It:* Activism for Teenagers. New York: Simon & Schuster Children's Publishing Division, 2004, pp.1-2.

4 Mark the main aim of the text.

- a. ◯ To describe the life of young activists from the United States.
- b. ◯ To present and discuss the main topic of the book – activism.

5 Mark the fragments below in which the author refers directly to the reader.

- a. ◯ "You know this, but it probably seems like the rest of the world doesn't."
- b. ◯ "You have the power to change them."
- c. ◯ "Don't wait until you're old enough to vote to take action."
- d. ◯ "This book is about activism, a word that is intimidating to a lot of people."
- e. ◯ "Some activists are agitators; some aren't."

6 Write a fragment from the text that shows the author's main viewpoint on teens and activism.

_____

_____

7 According to the text, "acting on your beliefs can happen in a lot of ways." Identify two examples given in the text to support this idea.

_____

_____

8 Read the fragments below and write (**F**) for **Fact** or (**O**) for **Opinion**.

- a. ◯ "Right now in the United States, twenty-six percent of the population is under eighteen."
- b. ◯ "I like to think of an activist as someone who acts on his or her beliefs and values."
- c. ◯ "Some are connected to larger organizations, and others do things solo."
- d. ◯ "But I bet that once you get going and see the changes you can make, you'll find yourself becoming more and more outspoken and committed."

Post-Reading

9 Discuss the questions below with a classmate.

- a. Are there things you want to change? If so, what are they? Do you believe you can help change them? Why (not)?
- b. In your opinion, what does an activist do?

Language in Use

Second conditional

Read the fragment from the text on page 52 and do **exercises** **1** and **2**.

> "Imagine what it would be like if you and everyone around you got to tell the world what you think."

1 Based on the situation above, mark the sentences that are true for you and write your own.

If I got to tell the world what I think, it would be…

a. ◯ "be proud of who you are."

b. ◯ "treat everybody with respect."

c. ◯ "fight for the things you care about."

d. ◯ "_____."

2 Mark the correct statement about the fragment.

a. ◯ It refers to a situation that is **real** and **possible in the future**.

b. ◯ It refers to a situation that is **not real** or **not probable now**.

3 Read this comic strip and mark the correct statements about it.

> I WONDER WHAT WOULD HAPPEN IF I WERE ALLERGIC TO CATS

> YOU'D HAVE TO MOVE OUT

Language Note

'd = would
wouldn't = would not

i.e. (= that is) = ou seja

a. ◯ Jon is allergic to cats.

b. ◯ Jon is talking about a hypothetical situation, i.e. that isn't real.

c. ◯ Garfield says that he wouldn't leave Jon's house if Jon were allergic to cats.

4 In the comic strip on page 54, Jon uses "I wonder" as a way of asking himself a question. Which one?

- a. ◇ Jon: "What would happen if I were allergic to cats?"
- b. ◇ Jon: "What would happen if you were allergic to cats?"

5 Complete this table.

SECOND CONDITIONAL			
_____ + main verb in the past simple	,	_____ + main verb in the base form	
_____ + main verb in the base form		_____ + main verb in the past simple	

> **Language Note**
> We often use **were** instead of **was** after *if*. In a formal style, **were** is more common than **was**.

6 Complete these quotes about hypotheses. Use the **second conditional**.

a. "It's not just people in Hollywood: I'm sure everyone in the world thinks, 'What would be it like if I _____ (win) an Oscar?'" (Roman Coppola)

From: <www.brainyquote.com/quotes/roman_coppola_492092>. Accessed on: May 10, 2019.

> **Language Note**
> We can use **could** instead of **would** to mean "would be able to".

b. "If I could choose to have one superpower, I _____ (want) to be able to make everyone love everyone!" (Betsey Johnson)

From: <www.brainyquote.com/quotes/betsey_johnson_928198>. Accessed on: May 10, 2019.

c. "If I _____ (can adopt) any zoo animal, it _____ (be) a giraffe. I have always loved giraffes. They are so graceful and beautiful to watch." (Torrey DeVitto)

From: <www.brainyquote.com/quotes/torrey_devitto_958889>. Accessed on: May 10, 2019.

Go to **Language Reference** on **page 120**.

Language Note

What if = What would happen if

Oral Skills

1 These cartoons show four different hypothetical situations. In pairs, try to think of as many possibilities as you can for each cartoon. Use the **second conditional**.

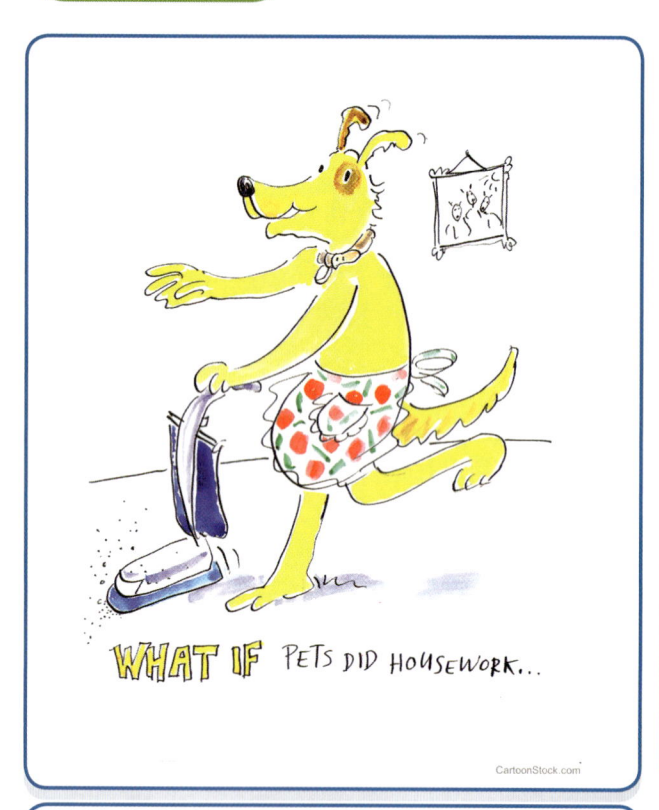

WHAT IF PETS DID HOUSEWORK...

WHAT IF FISH COULD CLIMB..

WHAT IF RAIN FELL SIDEWAYS...

WHAT IF SPONGES DIDN'T SUCK...

2 Before listening to the beginning of a talk by web cartoonist Randall Munroe, take a look at the cover of his book, *What if?* What is it about?

3 Now listen to Randall Munroe talk about the hypothetical questions he answers. Which questions is he talking about?

  a. ◯ The ones on his book.

  b. ◯ The ones on his website.

4 Listen to the recording again and mark the correct answers.

  a. How does Randall Munroe answer hypothetical questions?

   ◯ Using math, science and comics.

   ◯ Using mythology, science and cartoons.

  b. Which hypothetical question does he mention in the talk?

   ◯ "What would happen if the Earth and all terrestrial objects suddenly stopped spinning, but the atmosphere retained its velocity?"

   ◯ "What would happen if you tried to hit a baseball pitched at 90 percent of the speed of light?"

  c. Which picture illustrates the hypothetical question he mentions in the talk?

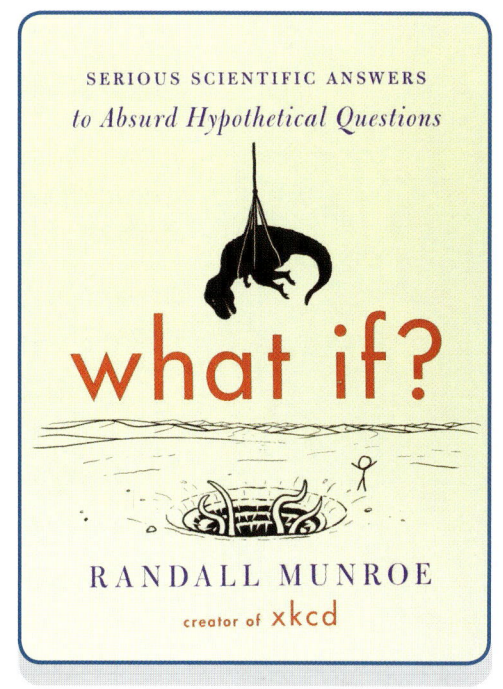

5 Listen to the recording once more and check your answers.

Writing

In this unit you have read cartoons about hypothetical situations on page 56. They are cartoons intended for humor that start with "What if". Visit <http://comics.azcentral.com> to find other examples of cartoons.

Based on the cartoons you have read in this unit, create your own cartoon showing a hypothetical situation.

- Follow these instructions to write your text.

    1. Imagine a funny situation that is not real or not likely to happen now.
    2. Work on the visual part of your cartoon.
    3. Add captions or speech bubbles to your cartoon. Like the cartoons on page 56, it can bring a sentence that starts with "What if".
    4. Exchange cartoons with a classmate and discuss them. Take into consideration the following:
        a. Does the combination of visual and verbal elements work? Do they help make the cartoon funny?
        b. Are all the words spelled correctly?
    5. Make the necessary corrections.
    6. Write the final version of your cartoon.

It is time to share your cartoon with your classmates and other people. You can also publish it on the school's website/blog. Based on people's reactions to your text, you can continue to improve it.

ENGLISH 4 LIFE

Read this comic strip and do **exercises 1** and **2**.

> **Panel 1:** WHAT IF WE COULD SEE INTO THE FUTURE, GARFIELD?
> **Panel 2:** EVEN JUST FIVE YEARS INTO THE FUTURE... WHAT WOULD WE SEE?
> **Panel 3:** PROBABLY THIS, AND HOPEFULLY WITH A FRESHER POT OF COFFEE

1 What's Garfield's answer to Jon's hypothetical question?

a. ◯ He believes things would be completely different.

b. ◯ He believes things would be just about the same.

2 What would be your answer to Jon's question ("What if we could see into the future?")?

_____

_____

3 In "Even just five years", **even** is used to emphasize the future time expression "just five years". Focus on these idioms with *even* in **bold** and mark the correct alternatives. Make inferences.

a. In "We'll get there, **even if** it takes five or ten years.", **even if** means

◯ no matter if. ◯ at the same time as.

b. In "**Even as** I left home it started raining.", **even as** means

◯ despite that. ◯ at the same time as.

c. In "We had a terrible fight yesterday. **Even so**, we still like each other.", **even so** means

◯ as a result. ◯ despite that.

Language Note

We use **even**:
- before a noun (e.g. <u>Even</u> Garfield can see into the future);
- before a verb (e.g. Jon <u>even</u> asked Garfield a hypothetical question);
- after an auxiliary verb (e.g. Garfield can <u>even</u> drink coffee).

Challenge!

In "Even though he's 40, he is childish at times.", what does **even though** mean?

✓ ✗

Extra Challenge!

In "They gave us no explanation, even less an apology.", what does **even less** mean?

✓ ✗

Play 'n' Learn 2

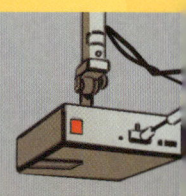

Games

It's time to challenge a classmate to a game about **conditionals**. Follow the instructions, play 'n' learn!

INSTRUCTIONS
1. Each student plays this game at a time.
2. The aim is to make as many sentences as possible within 2 minutes.
3. In each turn, players have 2 minutes to complete up to ten conditional sentences.
4. The player with the highest number of complete conditional sentences is the winner.

FIRST ROUND (FIRST CONDITIONAL)

1. I will hang out with my friends on the weekend if…
2. If it rains next Saturday, …
3. I will learn English faster if…
4. If I sleep late tonight, …
5. I won't watch TV today if…
6. If I don't exercise regularly, …
7. My English teacher will be happy if…
8. What will happen if…?
9. I'll be angry if…
10. I'll be surprised if…

1. If I could have any animal as a pet, …
2. The world would be a much better place if…
3. If I could live anywhere in the world, …
4. If I were famous for 24 hours, …
5. If I were a superhero/superheroine, …
6. If I had three wishes, …
7. If I could speak another language, …
8. What would happen if…?
9. I'd be very upset if…
10. I'd be really happy if…

SECOND ROUND
(SECOND CONDITIONAL)

TEST (UNITS 3 AND 4)

1 Use the **first conditional** to complete these quotes.

a. "If you change nothing, nothing _____ (change)." (Rajkummar Rao)

From: <www.indiatoday.in/movies/bollywood/story/rajkummar-rao-newton-official-entry-to-oscars-2018-interview-1050174-2017-09-22>. Accessed on: May 20, 2019.

b. "If you run from technology, it _____ (chase) you." (Robert M. Pirsig)

From: <www.cbc.ca/radio/ideas/the-motorcycle-is-yourself-revisiting-zen-and-the-art-of-motorcycle-maintenance-1.2914205>. Accessed on: May 20, 2019.

c. "If you _____ (not follow) your dream, who will?" (Emeril Lagasse)

From: <www.ecpi.edu/blog/why-did-you-become-a-chef-culinary-greats-talk-about-their-inspiration>. Accessed on: May 20, 2019.

d. "If every day is an awakening, you _____ (never grow) old. You will just keep growing." (Gail Sheehy)

From: <www.today.com/popculture/naomi-judd-dont-dread-growing-older-wbna16525237>. Accessed on: May 20, 2019.

awakening = despertar

chase = perseguir

SCORE: _____ / 24 (6 each)

2 Complete the sentences with the expressions in the box.

free/spare time • kill time • make time • right on time • take your time • waste time

a. There's no need to hurry. _____!

b. Don't _____ on what's not important.

c. Do you often watch TV in your _____?

d. I arrived there exactly at noon. That was _____.

e. I'm busy now, but I'll try to _____ to talk to you later.

f. I usually _____ on the Internet while waiting for the school bus.

SCORE: _____ / 24 (4 each)

3 Match the columns and find out four quotes about hypothetical situations.

a. "I would work every day ○   ○ I would be an eagle."

b. "If it were not for hopes, ○   ○ if I could."

c. "If I were an animal, ○   ○ I would rather have birds than airplanes."

d. "If I had to choose, ○   ○ the heart would break."

From: <www.latimes.com/archives/la-xpm-1988-01-21-vw-37478-story.html>; <www.brainyquote.com/quotes/thomas_fuller_133087>; <www.thedailystar.net/the-star/jamie-foxx-1382>; <http://movies2.nytimes.com/books/98/09/27/specials/lindbergh-conservationist.html>. Accessed on: May 20, 2019.

SCORE: _____ / 16 (4 each)

4 Use the **first** or the **second conditional** to complete these sentences.

a. If I got up earlier, I _____ (get) to school on time.

b. You'll learn English quicker if you _____ (practice) it every day.

c. If you trusted me, I _____ (can help) you.

d. What would you do if you _____ (be) invisible?

e. The world would be a much better place if everyone _____ (respect) each other.

f. They'll come if they _____ (not be) busy.

SCORE: _____ / 36 (6 each)

SCORE: _____ / 100

Go to **My Achievements** on page 65.

Play 'n' Learn 2 **63**

Project

TASK

In small groups, write a short biography about a respected Brazilian scientist. Groups should choose people from different research areas. Then, gather all the texts you and your classmates created to make a poster and share it among teachers, family members, friends, and other people from your community.

Some examples:

MAYANA ZATZ

Born in 1947, she is a Brazilian molecular biologist and geneticist.

She currently works as a professor at the University of São Paulo.

She is best known for her work with genetic counseling in families that were carriers of neuromuscular diseases.

▶ On the Web

Mayana Zatz

◂ http://livro.pro/izn73y ▸

(Acesso em: 20 maio 2019).

MIGUEL NICOLELIS

Born in 1961, he is a Brazilian scientist and physician.

He currently works as a professor at Duke University.

He is best known for his pioneering studies of brain machine interfaces and neuroprosthetics in human patients and non-human primates.

▶ On the Web

Miguel Nicolelis

◂ http://livro.pro/8jxb9w ▸

(Acesso em: 20 maio 2019).

Evaluating

Answer the questions below to evaluate the development of the project.

a. What have you learned from the project?

b. Did you have any difficulties? If so, what helped you overcome them?

c. Would you do anything differently? If so, what? Why?

My Achievements

Go back to **Unit 3** and **Unit 4** and check how many ticks (✓) you have. Use the table below to help you count the total number of ticks.

UNIT 3	CHALLENGE!	EXTRA CHALLENGE!
page 41		
page 49		
UNIT 4	**CHALLENGE!**	**EXTRA CHALLENGE!**
page 51		
page 59		

TOTAL NUMBER OF TICKS: _____ /8

Check what you get:

- **1 - 2 ticks** = 1 sticker (a clock app)
- **3 - 5 ticks** = 2 stickers (a clock app and a calculator app)
- **6 - 8 ticks** = 3 stickers (a clock app, a calculator app and a camera app)

Find your stickers in the **Stickers** section and place them on page 144.

Based on your total score in **Test (Units 3 and 4)**, see what you get:

- **60 to 79** = a bronze medal sticker
- **80 to 89** = a silver medal sticker
- **90 to 100** = a golden medal sticker

Find your sticker in the Stickers section and place it here.

PLACE YOUR STICKER HERE.

How do you feel about your **commitment** and **participation** in classes? Consider the development of the four skills (reading, writing, listening and speaking).

Find your sticker in the **Stickers** section and place it above.

UNIT 5
Fact or fake?

Learning Objectives

- to talk about evaluating information on the web;
- to use word groups to learn vocabulary;
- to use the **modal verbs may/might**;
- to explore **mind maps**.

Which photos on this page are actually fake?
In your opinion, is it easy to identify fake images on the Internet?

Getting Started

Word groups

1 On page 66 you could find some examples of fake photos. **Fake news** is another term that has become popular over the last years. Complete the mind map below with the words/expressions in the box.

> button • digital devices • fake news • link • scrollbar • to click • to drag and drop • to scroll

Mind map:
- smartphone, computer, tablet → **digital devices** → INTERNET VOCABULARY
- elements of a website → menu, __, __, __
- to browse, __, __, __ → actions performed
- __ → clickbait, satire, conspiracy theory (→ **fake news**)

Pronunciation Note

Listen to two different forms of pronouncing the word **news** and repeat them.

/nu:z/ (US)
/nju:z/ (UK)

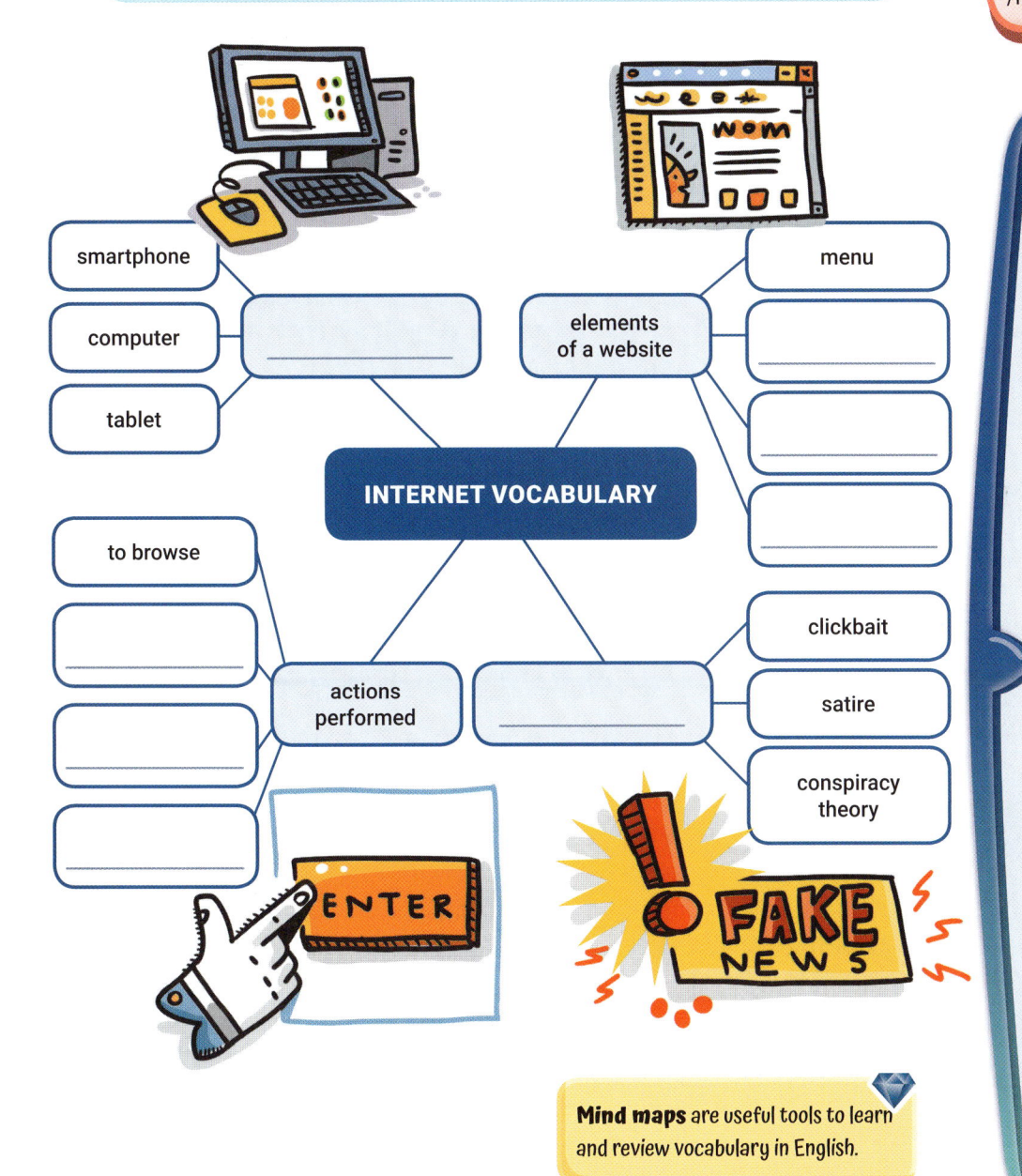

Challenge!

Add another item to "digital devices" in the mind map from *exercise 1*.

Extra Challenge!

Add another item to "actions performed" in the mind map from *exercise 1*.

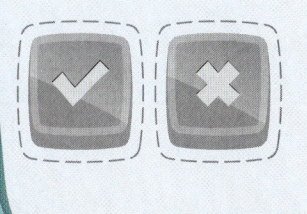

Mind maps are useful tools to learn and review vocabulary in English.

2 Listen to the words from the mind map and check your answers.

Unit 5

Reading Comprehension

Pre-Reading

1 Before reading the text, focus on its **layout** and **title** to answer the questions.

a. What do you expect to read about?
_____

b. How does the text address its subject: in an academic or practical way?
_____

Reading

Language Note

News is an *uncountable noun*, i.e. it has no plural.

2 Read the text below to check your predictions.

www.dailymail.co.uk/wires/ap/article-4218740/Fake-news-Tips-distinguish-real-thing.html

Fake news: Tips on how to distinguish it from the real thing

By ASSOCIATED PRESS
PUBLISHED: 14:42 BST, 13 February 2017 | UPDATED: 14:43 BST, 13 February 2017

Teachers from elementary school through college are instructing students on how to decipher fact from fiction when it comes to online news, after an election season that saw made-up stories abound. Some of their lessons:

- URL look odd? That "com.co" ending on an otherwise authentic-looking website is a red flag. When in doubt, click on the "contact" and "about" links to see where they lead. A major news organization probably isn't headquartered in a house.
- Does it make you mad? False reports often target emotions with claims of outlandish spending or unpatriotic words or deeds. If common sense tells you it can't be true, it may not be.
- If it's real, other news sites are likely reporting it.
- How is the writing? Caps lock and multiple exclamation points don't have a place in most real newsrooms.
- Who are the writers and the people in the story? Google names for clues to see if they are legitimate, or not.
- What are fact-checking sites like Snopes.com and FactCheck.org finding?
- It might be satire. Sometimes foolish stories aren't really meant to fool.
- Think twice before sharing. Today, everyone is a publisher.

From: <www.dailymail.co.uk/wires/ap/article-4218740/Fake-news-Tips-distinguish-real-thing.html>.
Accessed on: May 10, 2019.

---

be headquartered in = ser sediada(o) em

clue = pista

deed = ato, feito

odd/outlandish = estranho(a)

▶ On the Web

Identify Fake News
◂ http://livro.pro/wi7oyq ▸
(Acesso em: 10 maio 2019).

3 Mark the main objective of the text.

a. ◇ To present the consequences of fake news in today's world.

b. ◇ To share practical tips on differentiating fake news from real ones.

4 Complete this mind map with words and expressions from the text.

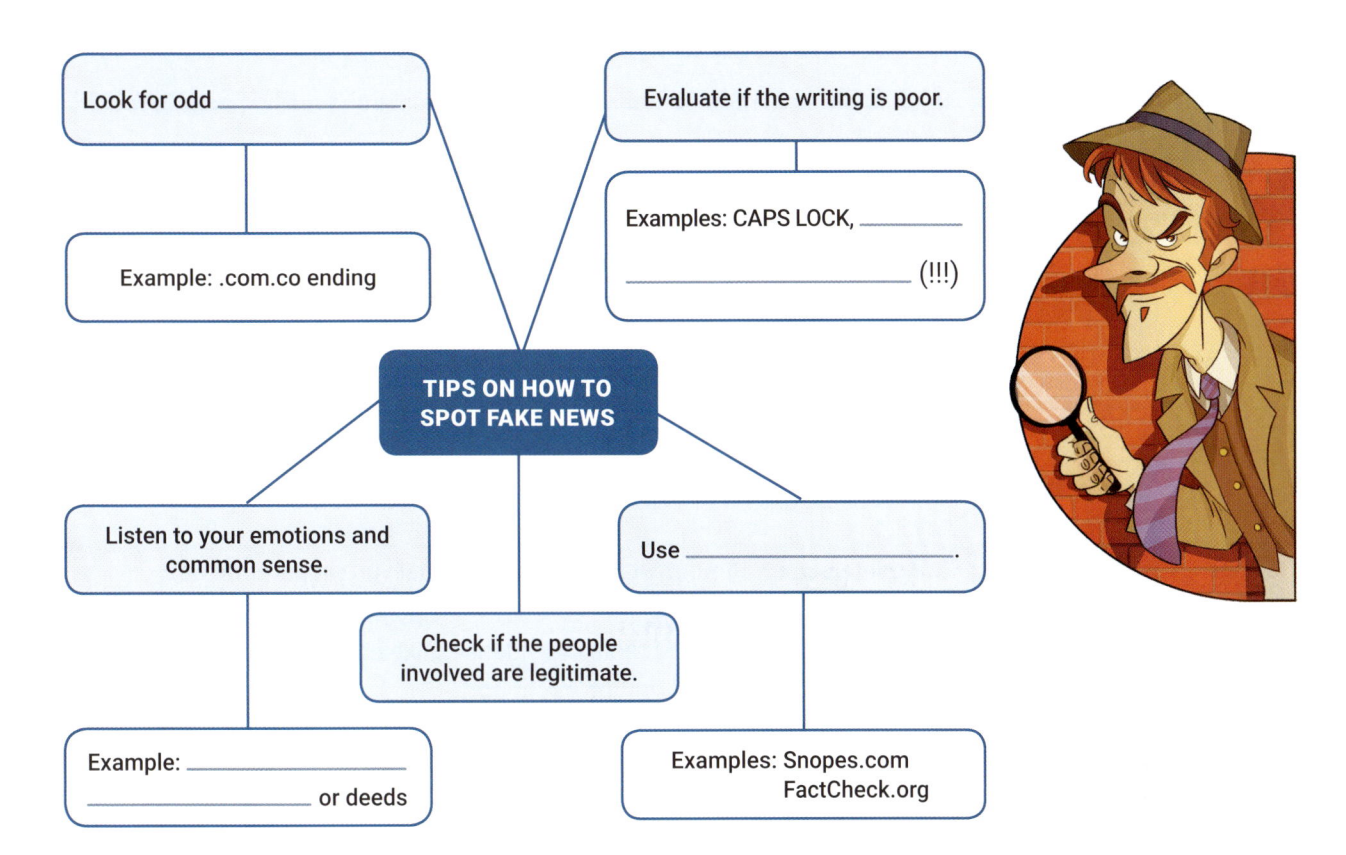

- Look for odd _____.
  - Example: .com.co ending
- Evaluate if the writing is poor.
  - Examples: CAPS LOCK, _____ _____ (!!!)
- Listen to your emotions and common sense.
- Use _____.
  - Examples: Snopes.com FactCheck.org
- Check if the people involved are legitimate.
  - Example: _____ _____ or deeds

TIPS ON HOW TO SPOT FAKE NEWS

5 Find a fragment in the text that is equivalent in meaning to each expression.

a. To differentiate fact from fake.

_____

b. A sign of danger.

_____

Post-Reading

6 Discuss the questions below with a classmate.

a. Do you think it is important for teachers to instruct students to distinguish fact from fiction when it comes to online news? Why (not)?

b. In your opinion, how can fake news impact on our everyday life? In small groups, make a list of possible consequences of fake news. Then, share your list with other classmates and get to know different viewpoints on the same topic.

Language in Use

Modal verbs: may/might

1 Read the fragments from the text on page 68 and mark the correct alternatives.

I. "If common sense tells you it can't be true, it **may** not be."

II. "It **might** be satire. Sometimes foolish stories aren't really meant to fool."

a. In fragment **I**, "it may not be" is equivalent in meaning to

◇ certainly it isn't. ◇ possibly it isn't.

b. In fragment **II**, "It might be satire" is equivalent in meaning to

◇ Certainly, it is satire. ◇ Possibly, it is satire.

c. We use **may** and **might** to say that things are

◇ *possible* – perhaps they are (not) true.

◇ *certain* – they are (not) true.

> **Language Note**
>
> We use modal verbs (*may*, *might* etc.) **before** the main verb in the base form.

2 Complete each fragment with the correct modal verb in parentheses.

a. "If you can't find any facts or evidence, take care – this _____ be a fake news story." (might/might not)

b. "If you think a story _____ be fake news, then do more research." (might/might not)

c. "False information _____ then be disseminated in various ways: (unwittingly or deliberately) shared on social media, amplified by journalists […]." (may/may not)

d. "Sometimes reporters or journalists _____ publish a story with unreliable information or without checking all of the facts which can mislead audiences." (may/may not)

e. "Experts can point you to research you _____ find on your own, and they often give important context to research you already found." (might/might not)

From: <https://libguides.rug.nl/c.php?g=660469&p=4714153>; <https://libguides.rug.nl/c.php?g=660469&p=4664047>; <https://libguides.rug.nl/c.php?g=660469&p=4664050>. Accessed on: May 10, 2019.

3 Complete the text with the sentences/clauses in the box.

> This may be a critique on a topic • The information may be accurate •
> The information may be entirely fabricated •
> These websites may intentionally misinterpret facts

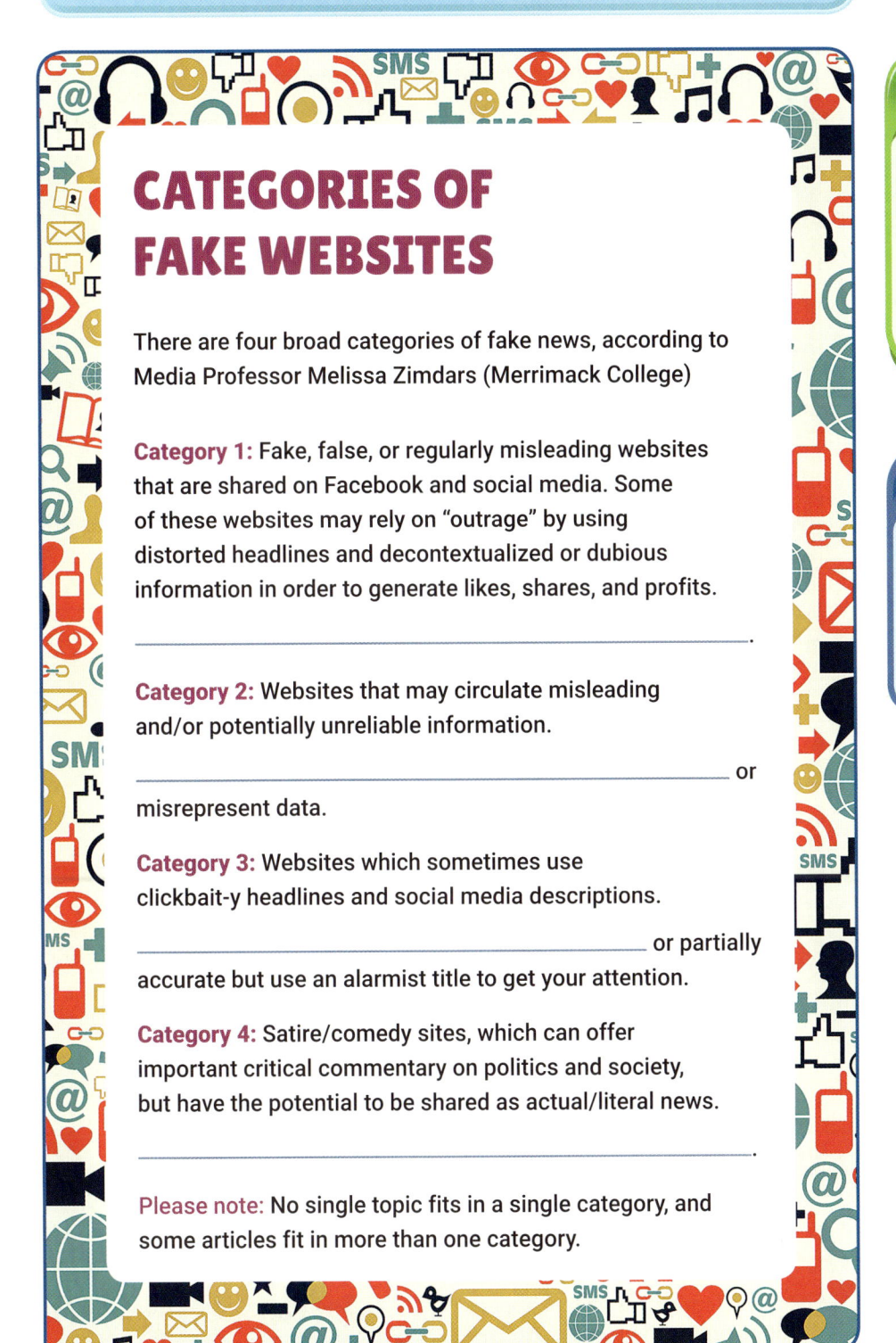

CATEGORIES OF FAKE WEBSITES

There are four broad categories of fake news, according to Media Professor Melissa Zimdars (Merrimack College)

Category 1: Fake, false, or regularly misleading websites that are shared on Facebook and social media. Some of these websites may rely on "outrage" by using distorted headlines and decontextualized or dubious information in order to generate likes, shares, and profits.

_____.

Category 2: Websites that may circulate misleading and/or potentially unreliable information.
_____ or misrepresent data.

Category 3: Websites which sometimes use clickbait-y headlines and social media descriptions.
_____ or partially accurate but use an alarmist title to get your attention.

Category 4: Satire/comedy sites, which can offer important critical commentary on politics and society, but have the potential to be shared as actual/literal news.
_____.

Please note: No single topic fits in a single category, and some articles fit in more than one category.

From: <https://libguides.rug.nl/c.php?g=660469&p=4664048>. Accessed on: May 10, 2019.

Language Note

<u>de</u>contextualized = not contextualized

<u>mis</u>leading = leading incorrectly

<u>un</u>reliable = not reliable

▶ On the Web

What Is Fake News

◄ http://livro.pro/bxj3yz ▶

(Acesso em: 10 maio 2019).

Go to **Language Reference** on **page 120**.

Oral Skills

1 Read this mind map and get to know how other forms of misinformation are used as fake news. Then, discuss the questions below with your classmates.

HOW OTHER FORMS OF MISINFORMATION ARE WEAPONIZED INTO FAKE NEWS

satire — when deceptively packaged as a legitimate news story

clickbait — when containing fabrications and packaged as a legitimate news story

propaganda — when containing fabrications and packaged as a legitimate news story

conspiracy theory — when packaged as a legitimate news story

misleading or out-of-context information — when also serving as support for fabrications

mediamatters.org

From: <https://libguides.uky.edu/breakingnews/weaponizedinfo>. Accessed on: May 10, 2019.

> propaganda = ideias, geralmente tendenciosas ou parciais, divulgadas a fim de influenciar as opiniões das pessoas.

▶ On the Web

How to Spot Fake News

◄ http://livro.pro/wveu8u ►

(Acesso em: 10 maio 2019).

a. Do you click on clickbait links often? When does it usually happen?

b. Which websites do you visit regularly? Are any of them satire sites, i.e. sites that use humor to expose and criticize people?

c. Do you see a lot of propaganda shared in your social media feeds? If so, what do you often do?

d. Do you regularly look for viral posts (videos, photos, articles)? How often do you share them on social media?

e. In your opinion, do you feel prepared to spot fake news? Why (not)?

2 Listen to the beginning of a radio program in which its host, Sarah McCammon, refers to a new study about fake news. Mark the item that correctly refers to the findings of the study.

a. ◯ Younger Americans shared the most fake news.

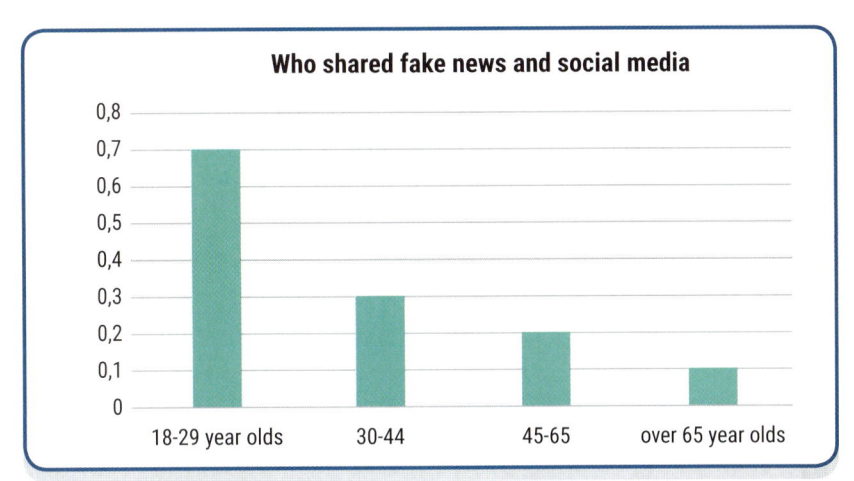

Who shared fake news and social media

Age group	Value
18-29 year olds	0.7
30-44	0.3
45-65	0.2
over 65 year olds	0.1

b. ◯ Older Americans shared the most fake news.

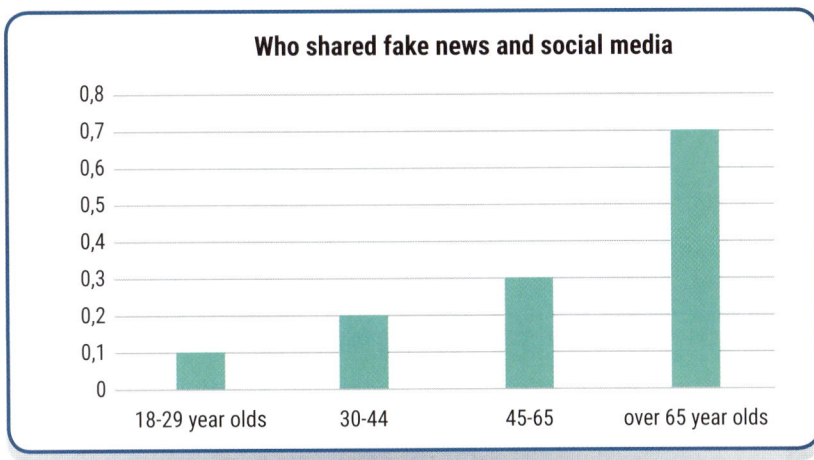

Who shared fake news and social media

Age group	Value
18-29 year olds	0.1
30-44	0.2
45-65	0.3
over 65 year olds	0.7

Source: <www.effinghamdailynews.com/news/elderly-conservatives-shared-more-facebook-fakery-in/article_4b2e8962-cd7a-57e1-afc8-37a5982b35af.html>. Accessed on: May 23, 2019.

3 Listen to the recording again and mark what Sarah McCammon mentions about the study.

a. ◯ The study was conducted by Princeton and New York Universities.

b. ◯ People like your great aunt or uncle are more likely to share fake news on social media.

c. ◯ Sarah McCammon's next guest is one of the authors of the study, professor Andy Guess.

d. ◯ Andy Guess is an assistant professor of politics and public affairs at New York University.

4 Listen to the recording once more and check your answers.

Writing

In this unit you have read mind maps on pages 67, 69 and 72. A mind map is a diagram that displays information visually and it is often created around a central idea or topic. The mind map on page 67 is a visual way to organize vocabulary. The second mind map was created as a tool to highlight the main ideas from the text on page 68. The third one (on page 72) was created around the different forms of fake news. Visit <https://mindmapsunleashed.com/10-really-cool-mind-mapping-examples-you-will-learn-from> to find other examples of mind maps.

- Based on the mind maps you have read in this unit, create your own mind map to give people useful tips on how to spot fake news.

Follow these instructions to write your text.

1. Place the central idea "tips for spotting fake news" in the center of the page. It is the starting point of your mind map.
2. Draw some lines or arrows from the central idea.
3. Try to get useful tips on the main topic and write down what comes to mind. Use meaningful keywords to write the tips. Reviewing the categories of fake websites presented on page 71 may bring you some ideas.
4. Expand your mind map. Try to flow from one idea into another. The beauty of mind maps is that you can continually add new ideas.
5. Include a picture or drawing to illustrate your mind map.
6. Exchange texts with a classmate and discuss them. Take into consideration the following:
    a. Does the use of colors and images make the mind map visually attractive?
    b. Are all the words spelled correctly?
7. Make the necessary corrections.
8. Create the final version of your mind map. You can draw it by hand or use an online resource such as <bubbl.us> or <mindmapfree.com>.

It is time to share your mind map with your classmates and other people. You can also publish it on the school's website/blog or a trusted travel website/blog. Based on people's reactions to your text, you can continue to improve it.

ENGLISH 4 LIFE

1 Read this cartoon and answer the questions.

a. Why is the man sitting on a tree?
_____
_____
_____
_____

b. In your opinion, is the man sitting on a tree an Internet addict? Why (not)?
_____
_____
_____
_____

2 **Wifi** is an Internet-related word which is widely used in Portuguese. You can find other Internet-related words in the word cloud below. Use six of them to complete the sentences (**a-f**).

a. _____ (abbreviation for *frequently asked question*) is a list of questions that people often ask about a particular thing or website and the answers to the questions.

b. _____ is advertising material you receive by e-mail without having asked for it.

c. _____ is a video blog. It can also be a verb – *to create and publish a video blog*.

d. _____ is a digital audio available on the Internet that can be downloaded and played on a computer or digital device.

e. _____ (abbreviation for *direct message*) is a private message that you send on a social media site, that can only be read by the person you send it to.

f. _____ is a place on a computer where email messages arrive.

Challenge!

What does **www** stand for?

Extra Challenge!

What does **URL** stand for?

Unit 5

UNIT 6 — Be a volunteer!

Learning Objectives

- to talk about volunteering;
- to use word groups to learn vocabulary;
- to use **modal verbs**: should/must/have to;
- to explore **infographics**.

Are you involved with any sort of volunteer work at your school? If so, what? How could you help people in your community?

Getting Started

Word groups

1 There is a mind map around the central idea of volunteering on page 76. Now complete the mind map below with the items in the box and learn more about the theme.

> It connects you to other people • It is good for your mind and body • Libraries or senior centers • Serve meals at a homeless shelter • Visit a nursing home • Where to volunteer?

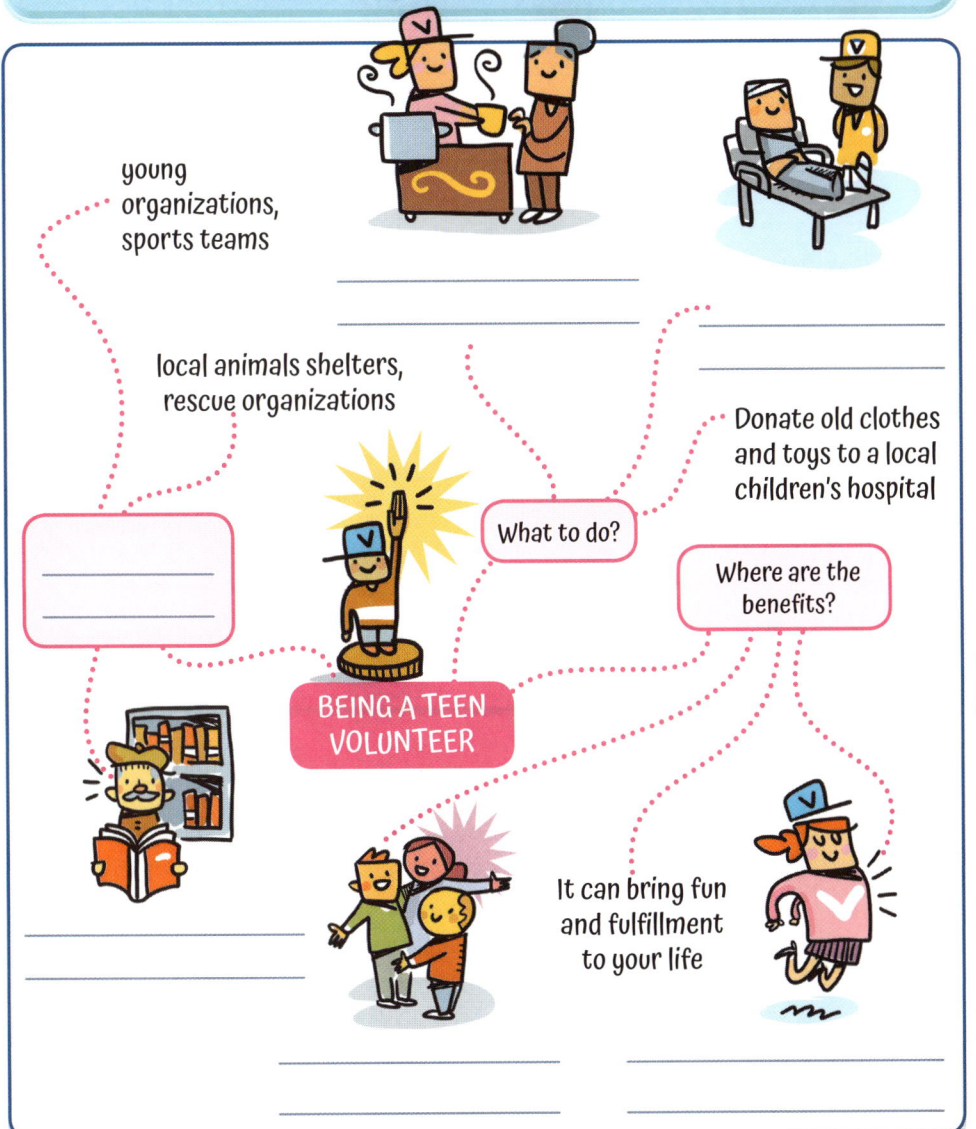

- young organizations, sports teams
- local animals shelters, rescue organizations
- Donate old clothes and toys to a local children's hospital
- What to do?
- Where are the benefits?
- **BEING A TEEN VOLUNTEER**
- It can bring fun and fulfillment to your life

2 Based on the mind map in **exercise 1**, what do you think you can do as a teen volunteer in your community?

On the Web

English Collocations Dictionary

◂ http://livro.pro/x8jymh ▸

(Acesso em: 10 maio 2019).

Challenge!

Add another item to "Where to volunteer?" in the mind map from **exercise 1**.

Extra Challenge!

Add another item to "What to do?" in the mind map from **exercise 1**.

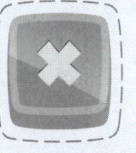

Unit 6

Reading Comprehension

Pre-Reading

1 Before reading the text, focus on its **title**, **subtitle** and **picture**. Then answer the questions.

a. What do you expect to read about in the text?

_____

b. Based on the subtitle, what two benefits does volunteering offer?

_____

Reading

2 Read the text below to check your predictions.

> worthwhile = que vale a pena

Volunteering and its Surprising Benefits
How Giving to Others Makes You Healthier and Happier

Why volunteer?

Volunteering offers vital help to people in need, worthwhile causes, and the community, but the benefits can be even greater for you, the volunteer. Volunteering and helping others can reduce stress, combat depression, keep you mentally stimulated, and provide a sense of purpose. While it's true that the more you volunteer, the more benefits you'll experience, volunteering doesn't have to involve a long-term commitment or take a huge amount of time out of your busy day. Giving in even simple ways can help those in need and improve your health and happiness. [...]

How much time should you volunteer?

Volunteering doesn't have to take over your life to be beneficial. In fact, research shows that just two to three hours per week, or about 100 hours a year, can confer the most benefits – to both you and your chosen cause. The important thing is to volunteer only the amount of time that feels comfortable to you. Volunteering should feel like a fun and rewarding hobby, not another chore on your to-do list. [...]

From: <www.helpguide.org/articles/healthy-living/volunteering-and-its-surprising-benefits.htm>. Accessed on: May 15, 2019.

3 Based on the text, mark the sentence about volunteering that is **not** true.

a. ◯ The more you volunteer, the more benefits you will have.

b. ◯ Volunteering requires a long-term commitment.

c. ◯ Two or three hours a week are enough to provide volunteers with benefits.

4 When talking about volunteering, the author mentions that "the benefits can be even greater for you, the volunteer." Identify four examples given in the text to support this idea.

_____

_____

_____

5 According to the text, "Volunteering doesn't have to take over your life to be beneficial." Identify a fragment in the text that shows some evidence for this view.

_____

_____

_____

6 Read the fragments below and write (**F**) for **Fact** or (**O**) for **Opinion**.

a. ◯ "In fact, research shows that just two to three hours per week, or about 100 hours a year, can confer the most benefits – to both you and your chosen cause."

b. ◯ "Volunteering should feel like a fun and rewarding hobby, not another chore on your to-do list."

Post-Reading

7 Discuss the questions below with a classmate.

a. The text brings up the idea that "giving to others makes you healthier and happier." Do you usually feel this way when you help others? How do you usually help at home?

b. According to the text, "Giving in even simple ways can help those in need and improve your health and happiness." In small groups, make a list of possible ways to help others in your local community. Then, share your list with other classmates and get to know different ideas on the same topic.

Language in Use

Modal verbs: should/must/have to

1 Read the fragments from the text on page 78 and mark the correct alternatives.

  I. "Volunteering **doesn't have to** take over your life to be beneficial."

  II. "Volunteering **should** feel like a fun and rewarding hobby […]."

  III. "[…] volunteering **doesn't have to** involve a long-term commitment […]."

  IV. "How much time **should** you volunteer?"

  a. The sentence that is equivalent in meaning to fragment **I** is

  ◯ Volunteering can't take over your life to be beneficial.

  ◯ Volunteering doesn't need to take over your life to be beneficial.

  b. In fragments **I** and **III**, **not have to** expresses

  ◯ prohibition. ◯ lack of necessity.

  c. The sentence that is equivalent in meaning to fragment **II** is

  ◯ Volunteering needs to feel like a fun and rewarding hobby.

  ◯ It's recommended that volunteering feels like a fun and rewarding hobby.

  d. In fragments **II** and **IV**, **should** expresses

  ◯ advice, recommendation. ◯ necessity, obligation.

Read this cartoon and do **exercises** 2 and 3.

2 Mark the correct statements about the cartoon.

  a. ◯ The kids are playing video games.

  b. ◯ The challenges in this game involve being kind.

  c. ◯ This game doesn't offer varying levels of difficulty.

3 According to the character, players **must** perform acts of kindness in this game. What does **must** express?

a. ◇ Advice, recommendation.

b. ◇ Necessity, obligation.

> **Language Note**
> We use modal verbs (*must, should, (not) have to*, etc.) **before** the main verb in the base form.

4 Complete the "Meanings" column from the table with the items in the box as in the example.

> ~~prohibition~~ • advice/recommendation • lack of necessity/obligation • necessity/obligation

> **Language Note**
> **mustn't** = must not
> **shouldn't** = should not

	MODAL VERBS	EXAMPLES	MEANINGS
a.	have to/must	You **have to** be kind to everybody. You **must** be kind to everybody.	_____
b.	not have to	You **don't have to** volunteer for long hours.	_____
c.	mustn't	You **mustn't** enter this area.	*prohibition*
d.	should/shouldn't	Volunteering **should** be fun. Volunteering **shouldn't** be boring.	_____

5 Match the columns and get to know the difference between the words in **bold**.

a. You **mustn't** work here.   ◇ It means *you don't need to work here*.

b. You **don't have to** work here.   ◇ It means *you are prohibited from working here*.

> Peace Corps = Corpo da Paz (agência federal estadunidense independente, criada em 1961 para ajudar os países em desenvolvimento)

6 Complete each quote with the correct modal verb in parentheses.

a. "In the Peace Corps, the volunteer _____ (doesn't have to/must) be a fully developed, mature person. He _____ (has to/must not) join to run abroad or escape problems." (Sargent Shriver)

SARGENT SHRIVER. *Outlook for Corpsmen*: Army Could Be Better. Life. Mar. 17, 1961. p. 39.

b. "My mother and my father both believe you _____ (have to/mustn't) work hard and give back. That's why I was a volunteer firefighter, that's why I worked in a homeless shelter." (Thomas Kean, Jr.)

From: <www.washingtonpost.com/archive/lifestyle/2006/10/23/kean-on-politics-span-classbankheadnew-jerseys-political-scion-aims-to-make-a-name-for-himself-in-washingtonspan/83de1346-eef4-4400-8b2b-5d738443f070/?noredirect=on&utm_term=.5c246e09a46a>. Accessed on: May 15, 2019.

Go to **Language Reference** on page 121.

On the Web

Volunteering Can Help Mental Health

◄ http://livro.pro/7qsg9u ►

(Acesso em: 15 maio 2019).

Challenge!

Watch the video from the **On the Web** box. What mental illness did volunteering help Catherine Connolly deal with?

Extra Challenge!

Watch the video from the **On the Web** box. What animals does Catherine Connolly help as a volunteer?

Oral Skills

1. In your opinion, why do people volunteer?

2. In small groups, prepare a short speech about the health benefits of volunteering and present it to the whole class. Use elements from this infographic (e.g. statistics, facts) to help you make the presentation. You can also record it as a podcast and share it with other people.

Health Benefits of Volunteering

- Builds self-esteem
- Reduces stress
- Creates a sense of purpose
- Teaches caring
- Makes you happy

Researchers at the London School of Economics claim that volunteering creates the happiness effect. People were:

7% more likely to say they felt "very happy" if they volunteered monthly, **12%** if twice a month, and **16%** if they volunteered weekly.

Source: <www.healthfitnessrevolution.com/top-10-health-benefits-volunteering/>. Accessed on: May 31, 2019.

3 Listen to the beginning of a radio program. What is it about?

a. ◯ Volunteers are working to save homes and businesses from floods.

b. ◯ More and more companies are paying workers to volunteer on company time.

4 Listen to the recording again and mark the picture that shows the volunteer work described.

a. ◯　　　　　　　　　　　　b. ◯

5 Listen to the recording once more and take notes on its main ideas. Then, use your notes to help you mark the correct answers below.

a. What group of volunteers is mentioned in the recording?

　◯ A group of US business students.

　◯ A group of US Bank employees.

b. When do they work as volunteers?

　◯ Every Friday morning.　　◯ Every Sunday morning.

c. Who do they help?

　◯ Most of the people are kids and their moms.

　◯ Most of the people are homeless men.

d. How does Lisa Eriksson describe her experience as a volunteer?

　◯ As pretty emotional.　　◯ As happy and grateful.

6 Listen to the recording another time and check your answers.

Writing

In this unit you have read an infographic about the health benefits of volunteering on page 82. Infographics are visual presentations of information that use different elements (e.g. graphics, statistics, references) to display content. Visit <www.pinterest.com/initliveinc/volunteer-infographics/> to find other examples of infographics related to the topic.

- Based on the infographic you have read in this unit, write an infographic about volunteering. You can write about the benefits of volunteering, examples of volunteer work for teens, etc. Consider the school community (students, teachers, parents) as the target audience.

Follow these instructions to write your text.

1. Do research to gather information about volunteering. Look for reliable sources.
2. Check all the pieces of information you get (e.g. facts, statistics) and select the ones that are most relevant.
3. Write a draft of the text.
4. Look for potential images that illustrate the subject topic.
5. Place the text and images in a visually attractive configuration. Keep your infographic visual.
6. Exchange infographics with a classmate and discuss them. Take into consideration the following:

    a. Is the infographic suitable for the target audience?

    b. Is the information about the topic accurate?

    c. Do the pictures make the text more attractive?

7. Make the necessary corrections.
8. Create the final version of your infographic. You can use a computer to design it.

It is time to share your infographic with your classmates and other people. You can also publish it on the school's website/blog or on a non-profit organization's website. Based on people's reactions to your text, you can continue to improve it.

ENGLISH 4 LIFE

Read this comic strip and do **exercises 1** and **2**.

1 Mark the correct sentences about the comic strip. Make inferences.

a. ◯ Brad may work as a firefighter.

b. ◯ Brad decided to volunteer on Christmas.

c. ◯ Brad chose to be a volunteer Santa Claus.

d. ◯ Brad is comfortable in his Santa Claus costume.

2 Choose the dialog that refers to the situation portrayed in the comic strip.

a. ◯ Toni: You don't have to be a volunteer Santa Claus, Brad.

   Brad: You must be joking! Of course, I will.

b. ◯ Toni: You have to be a volunteer Santa Claus, Brad.

   Brad: You must be joking! I'm afraid I won't.

3 Mark the correct statements about the sentence "You must be joking!"

a. ◯ It shows that someone is very surprised.

b. ◯ It is equivalent to *You must be kidding!*

c. ◯ It is equivalent to *You can't be serious!*

d. ◯ It is a formal expression.

4 Are the sentences "Are you kidding?!" and "You must be kidding!" used in formal or informal situations?

___

Play 'n' Learn 3

Games

INSTRUCTIONS

It's time to play tic-tac-toe with a classmate. Draw an **X** or **0** over a number (**1-9**) when you make a sentence with the modal verb given. Talk about fake news. Don't forget to play 'n' learn!

ROUND 1
(Talking about fake news)

1 MAY	2 SHOULD	3 NOT HAVE TO
4 HAVE TO	5 MUST	6 MIGHT
7 MUST NOT	8 MIGHT NOT	9 SHOULD NOT

INSTRUCTIONS

It's time to play tic-tac-toe. Draw an **X** or **O** over a number (**1-9**) when you make a sentence with the modal verb given. Talk about volunteering. Don't forget to play 'n' learn!

ROUND 2
(Talking about volunteering)

1 HAVE TO	2 MUST	3 SHOULD
4 NOT HAVE TO	5 MUST NOT	6 SHOULD NOT
7 MAY	8 MIGHT	9 MIGHT NOT

TEST (UNITS 5 AND 6)

1 Complete the text with the correct modal verbs in parentheses.

What makes a news story fake?

1. **You can't verify its claims.** A fake news article may or _____ (might have/may not have) links in it tracing its sources; if it does, these links _____ (may lead/may not lead) to articles outside of the site's domain or _____ (may contain/may not contain) information pertinent to the article topic.

2. **Fake news appeals to emotion.** Fake news plays on your feelings - it makes you angry or happy or scared. This is to ensure you won't do anything as pesky as fact-checking.

3. **Authors usually aren't experts.** Most authors aren't even journalists, but paid trolls.

4. **It can't be found anywhere else.** If you look up the main idea of a fake news article, you _____ (might find/might not find) any other news outlet (real or not) reporting on the issue.

5. **Fake news comes from fake sites.** Did your article come from abcnews.com.co? Or Realnewsrightnowcom? These and a host of other URLs are fake news sites.

From: <https://libguides.uwf.edu/c.php?g=609513&p=4231011>. Accessed on: May 20, 2019.

SCORE: _____ / 20 (5 each)

2 Complete the text with the words in the box.

> might • may agree • may be called • may contextualize

Distinguish Opinion from Fact

Even news websites and programs have spaces or shows dedicated to people's opinions of news stories. In newspapers, these sections _____ :

- Editorials • Letters to the Editor • Op-Eds • Opinion

Opinion shows many times now dominate cable news sources. You _____ with the opinions presented, or they _____ the facts for you in a way that makes sense. However, realize they are presenting the facts in a way that meets their agenda and think for yourself: How _____ "the other side" present these same facts?

From: <https://libguides.uwf.edu/c.php?g=609513&p=4274530>. Accessed on: May 20, 2019.

SCORE: _____ / 20 (5 each)

3 Complete the sentences with words from the box. There is one extra word.

> DM • FAQ • podcast • spam • vlog

a. _____ is a video blog.

b. _____ is advertising material you receive by e-mail without having asked for it.

c. _____ is a digital audio available on the Internet that can be played on a computer or digital device.

d. _____ is a private message that you send on a social media site, that can only be read by the person you send it to.

SCORE: _____/ 8 (2 each)

4 Match the columns.

a. You **should** work here.   It means *you have to work here*.

b. You **must** work here.   It means *you don't need to work here*.

c. You **mustn't** work here.   It means *you are advised to work here*.

d. You **don't have to** work here.   It means *you are prohibited from working here*.

SCORE: _____/ 16 (4 each)

5 Put the words into the correct order to write sentences.

> paid staff = pessoal remunerado

a. volunteer? / should / teens / Why

_____

b. good / Volunteering / be / for body / may / and mind.

_____

c. might / Your / organizations. / you / to professional / expose/ volunteer work

_____

d. a volunteer / If you are / have to / its instructions. / at an organization, / you / follow

_____

e. of the beneficiaries / must / of the volunteering activity. / Volunteers / the rights / respect.

_____

f. should / Volunteers / be / for paid staff. / not / substitutes

_____

SCORE: _____/ 36 (6 each)   **TOTAL:** _____/ 100   Go to **My Achievements** on page 91.

Project

TASK

In pairs, write an acrostic poem about volunteering and select one or more images to illustrate it. In your poem, you can define volunteering or thank volunteers for their work. You can also talk about the reasons for volunteering. Then, gather all the acrostic poems created by you and your classmates to make a poster about volunteering and share them among teachers, family members, friends, and other people from your community. You can also publish your poems on the Internet. Be grateful and encourage people to volunteer!

An example:

VOLUNTEERS...

THREE CHEERS FOR VOLUNTEERS!

Very important people!
Outstanding!
Love to be helpful!
Understand children!
Needed for many things!
Teachers value them!
Enjoy helping children!
Enthusiastic adults!
Ready at a moment's notice!
Special people!

Thank you!

Source: <www.poemsearcher.com/topic/volunteer+appreciation#&gid=1&pid=3>. Accessed on: May 20, 2019.

> **On the Web**
>
> Poems to Thank Volunteers – Volunteers Are Priceless
>
> ◄ http://livro.pro/9metub ►
>
> (Acesso em: 20 maio 2019).

Evaluating

Answer the questions below to evaluate the development of the project.

a. What have you learned from the project?

b. Did you have any difficulties? If so, what helped you overcome them?

c. Would you do anything differently? If so, what? Why?

My Achievements

Go back to **Unit 5** and **Unit 6** and check how many ticks (✓) you have. Use the table below to help you count the total number of ticks.

UNIT 5	CHALLENGE!	EXTRA CHALLENGE!
page 67		
page 75		
UNIT 6	**CHALLENGE!**	**EXTRA CHALLENGE!**
page 77		
page 82		

TOTAL NUMBER OF TICKS: _____ /8

Check what you get:
- **1 - 2 ticks** = 1 sticker (an e-reader app)
- **3 - 5 ticks** = 2 stickers (an e-reader app and a browser app)
- **6 - 8 ticks** = 3 stickers (an e-reader app, a browser app and a music player app)

Find your stickers in the **Stickers** section and place them on page 144.

Based on your total score in **Test (Units 5 and 6)**, see what you get:
- **60 to 79** = a bronze medal sticker
- **80 to 89** = a silver medal sticker
- **90 to 100** = a golden medal sticker

Find your sticker in the **Stickers** section and place it here.

PLACE YOUR STICKER HERE.

How do you feel about your **commitment** and **participation** in classes? Consider the development of the four skills (reading, writing, listening and speaking).

Find your sticker in the **Stickers** section and place it above.

UNIT 7
Advertising and body image

Learning Objectives

- to talk about the impact of advertising;
- to learn vocabulary related to health problems;
- to use the present perfect (regular verbs);
- to explore advertising posters.

WE HAVE YOUR DAUGHTER. We are forcing her to throw up after every meal she eats. It's only going to get worse. — BULIMIA

Don't let a psychiatric disorder take your child.
The NYU Child Study Center is dedicated to giving children back their childhood by preventing, identifying, and treating psychiatric and learning disorders.
To learn more, call (888) 7-NYU-MED or visit AboutOurKids.org.

What is this advertising poster about? What is its main objective?

Getting Started

Health problems

weight (noun) = peso
weigh (verb) = pesar

1 The advertising poster on page 92 mentions a serious health problem – **bulimia**. Based on the text and what you know about it, mark the correct definition for this disorder.

- a. ◯ An eating disorder that involves eating non-food items such as hair, dirt or paint.
- b. ◯ An eating disorder in which a person eats large amounts of food and then vomits intentionally.
- c. ◯ An eating disorder in which a person does not eat, or eats too little, leading to dangerous weight loss.

2 Which alternative in **exercise 1** refers to **anorexia**, another eating disorder? _____

3 Complete the sentences with words and expressions from the picture as in the example.

(Word cloud around "eating disorder": body dysmorphia, media, control, anorexia, bulimia, depression, anxiety, low self-esteem, mental illness, perfectionism, guilt, peer pressure, picky eating, binge eating)

- a. _**Low self-esteem**_ is characterized by a lack of confidence and feeling badly about yourself.
- b. Examples of _____ include depression, anxiety and eating disorders.
- c. The state of feeling very unhappy and without hope for the future is known as _____ .
- d. _____ is when a person refuses food or eats the same food over and over again.
- e. Worrying a lot about a specific area of your body and comparing your looks with other people's can be signs of _____ .

4 Listen to the recording and check your answers.

On the Web

Eating Disorders Program

◂ http://livro.pro/f5w3hy ▸

(Acesso em: 15 maio 2019).

Challenge!

Write three examples of **eating disorders**.

Extra Challenge!

Write three examples of **mental illness**.

Reading Comprehension

Pre-Reading

1 Before reading the text, focus on its **title** and **subtitle**. Then circle the words and expressions you expect to find in the text.

body shape • eating disorders • low self-esteem • magazines • media • mental illness • models • societal trends

Reading

2 Read the text below to check your predictions.

Pronunciation Note

🔊 Listen to two different forms of pronouncing the word **advertisement** and repeat them.

/ˌædvərˈtaɪzmənt/ (US)

/ədˈvɜːtɪsmənt/ (UK)

---

ad (= advertisement) = anúncio, propaganda

average = média

witness = testemunhar

---

www.thebalancecareers.com/the-impact-of-advertising-on-body-image-4151839

The Impact of Advertising on Body Image

Can Today's Ads Be Harmful to Our Self-Esteem?

BY PAUL SUGGETT • Updated February 06, 2019

Advertising is often a reflection of pop culture and societal trends; however, it can also shape them. Over the last 20-30 years, we have witnessed a strong correlation between advertising and body image, and the effects can be devastating. While it mostly affects women and girls, men and boys are not immune.

Here are some statistics from Joel Miller's article on media and body image that may be shocking to read:

- On average, most models weigh 23% less than the average woman. Twenty years ago, this difference was a mere 8%.
- Problems with eating disorders have increased over 400% since 1970.
- Only 5% of US women fit the body type popularly portrayed in today's advertising.
- Sixty-nine percent of girls concurred that models found in magazines had a major influence on their concept of what a perfect body shape should look like. […]

The evidence shows links between advertising and negative body image and self-esteem in both sexes. So, what can be done? Unfortunately, not much without society demanding change.

From: <www.thebalancecareers.com/the-impact-of-advertising-on-body-image-4151839>. Accessed on: May 15, 2019.

3 Write down two adjectives that the author uses to describe the impact of advertising on body image.

_____

4 What strategy/evidence does the author use to show links between advertising and negative body image?

_____

_____

5 Read the fragments below and write (**F**) for **Fact** or (**O**) for **Opinion**.

a. ◇ "On average, most models weigh 23% less than the average woman."

b. ◇ "Only 5% of US women fit the body type popularly portrayed in today's advertising."

c. ◇ "So, what can be done? Unfortunately, not much without society demanding change."

6 Mark the correct alternatives.

a. In "however, it can also shape them", the linking word **however** introduces an

◇ addition. ◇ opposition.

b. In "that may be shocking to read", the modal verb **may** expresses

◇ certainty. ◇ possibility.

c. In "Sixty-nine percent of girls concurred that models", **concurred** means

◇ agreed. ◇ disagreed.

Pronunciation Note

🔊 Listen to the recording and notice how the words in **bold** are pronounced.

a. How much do you **weigh**? About 60 kilos.

b. **Weight** refers to how heavy a person or a thing is.

c. **Height** refers to how tall a person or a thing is.

Post–Reading

7 Discuss the questions below with a classmate.

a. Do you think today's ads can be harmful to our self-esteem? Why (not)?

b. In your opinion, how can we demand change in advertising so that it does not impact on our body image and self-esteem?

Unit 7

Language in Use

Present perfect (regular verbs)

Read these fragments from the text on page 94 and do **exercises 1** and **2**.

I. "Over the last 20-30 years, we **have witnessed** a strong correlation between advertising and body image [...]"

II. "Problems with eating disorders **have increased** over 400% since 1970."

1 Answer the questions.

a. Which time expression is used in fragment **I**?

_____

b. Which time expression is used in fragment **II**?

_____

2 Mark the correct answers.

a. Which sentence is equivalent in meaning to fragment **II**?

◯ Problems with eating disorders have increased over 400% in 1970.

◯ Problems with eating disorders have increased over 400% for more than 40 years.

b. What kind of time expressions are used in the two fragments?

◯ Finished-time expressions.

◯ Unfinished-time expressions.

c. Why is the present perfect used in the two fragments?

◯ To talk about finished actions in the past.

◯ To talk about actions that have continued up to the present.

d. What is the structure of the present perfect?

◯ Be + past participle.

◯ Have/has + past participle.

e. What do the main verbs in bold have in common?

◯ They are **regular verbs** in the past participle.

◯ They are **irregular verbs** in the past participle.

> **Language Note**
>
> **Regular verbs** in the past participle end in **-ed**.

3 Circle the time expressions used in these sentences.

  a. The incidence of eating disorders has increased dramatically lately.

  b. They've recently recovered from anorexia nervosa.

Language Note
've = have

4 Complete these statistics about eating disorders with the correct form of the regular verbs in parentheses. Use the **present perfect**.

  a. It is estimated that 1.0% to 4.2% of women _____ from anorexia in their lifetime. (suffer)

  b. The number of people diagnosed with eating disorders _____ by 15 per cent since 2000. (increase)

  c. [...] at least for the last two decades, the rates of new diagnoses of anorexia and bulimia _____ relatively stable. (remain)

From: <www.eatingdisorderhope.com/information/statistics-studies>; <www.anorexiabulimiacare.org.uk/about/statistics>; <www.nationaleatingdisorders.org/statistics-research-eating-disorders>. Accessed on: May 15, 2019.

5 Mark the sentence that correctly refers to this graph.

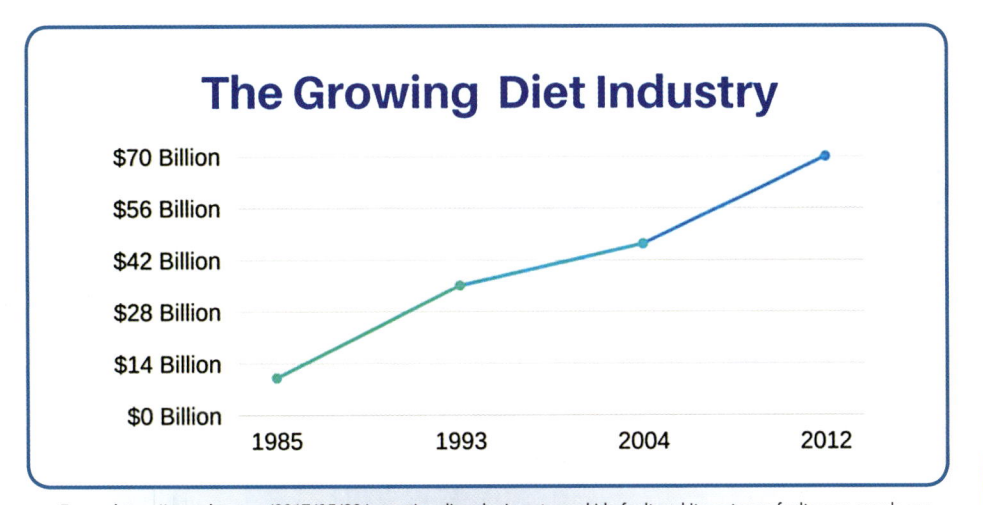

The Growing Diet Industry

(Graph showing values from 1985 to 2012, rising from near $0 Billion to about $70 Billion)

From: <https://more-love.org/2017/05/23/an-eating-disorder-is-not-your-kids-fault-and-its-not-your-fault-more-people-are-getting-eating-disorders-than-ever-this-is-bigger-than-you-your-child-and-your-family/>. Accessed on: May 15, 2019.

Language Note
hasn't = has not
haven't = have not

  a. ◯ The diet industry has increased since 1985.

  b. ◯ The diet industry hasn't increased for over 30 years.

6 Complete these statements with words used in the sentences in **exercise 5**.

  a. In negative sentences, we use haven't/ _____ + past participle.

  b. We use _____ to introduce a *period of time* (e.g. over 30 years).

  c. We use _____ to introduce a *starting point* (e.g. 1985).

Go to **Language Reference** on page 121.

Oral Skills

Language Note

In interrogative sentences, we use: **Have/Has + subject + past participle**. Notice that **ever** is used in the questions for emphasis. It means *at any time*.

1 How does advertising impact on your life? Answer the questions below and then interview a classmate.

	YOU		CLASSMATE	
	Yes	No	Yes	No
Has TV advertising ever influenced your choice when buying a product? If so, which one(s)?				
Have you ever started a diet to look similar to someone else in a magazine ad? If so, who?				
Have you ever compared your looks with someone else's in an ad? What did you compare?				
Has a celebrity ever influenced you to do something? If so, what?				

2 In small groups, prepare a short speech about body image and present it to the whole class. Use elements from this infographic (e.g. statistics, facts, tips) to help you make the presentation. You can also record it as a podcast and share it with other people.

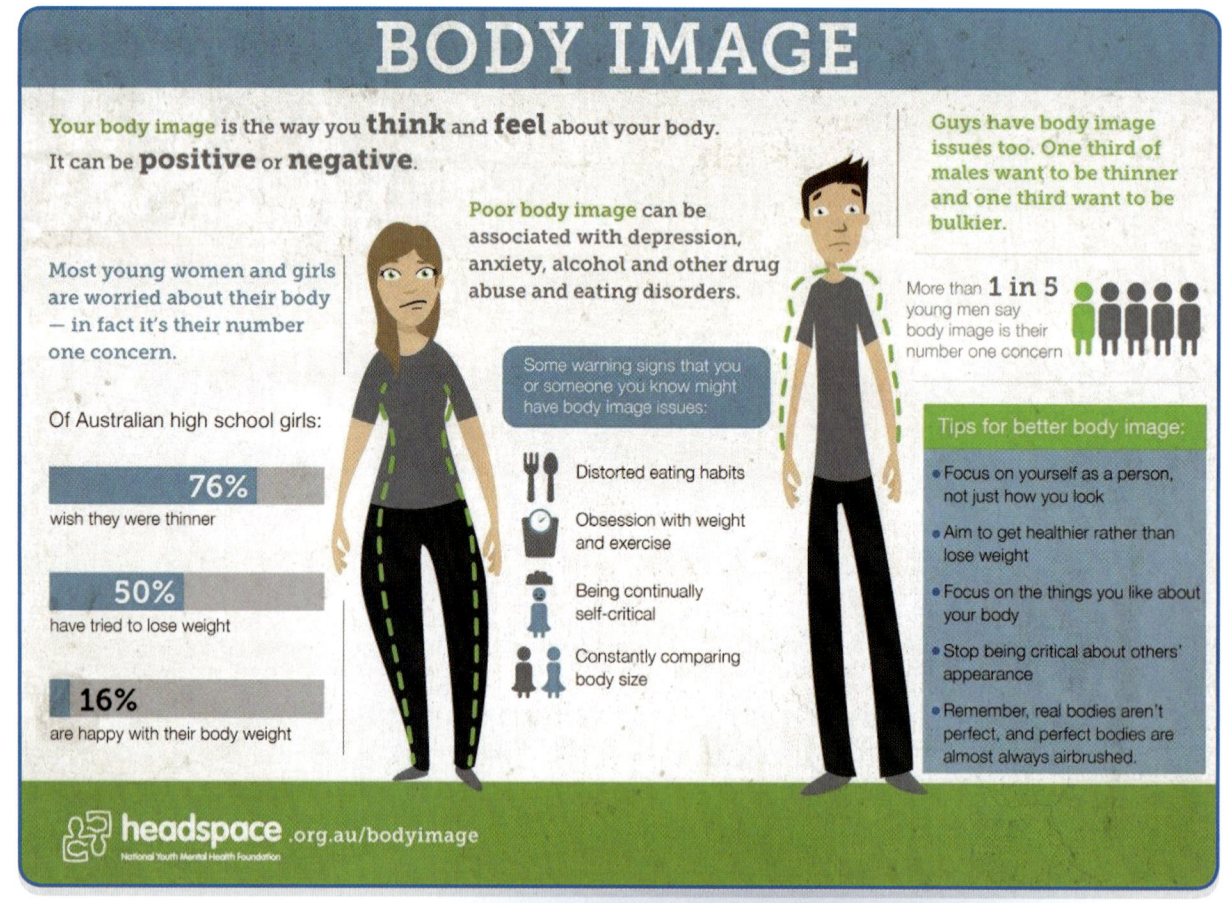

BODY IMAGE

Your body image is the way you **think** and **feel** about your body. It can be **positive** or **negative**.

Most young women and girls are worried about their body — in fact it's their number one concern.

Of Australian high school girls:
- **76%** wish they were thinner
- **50%** have tried to lose weight
- **16%** are happy with their body weight

Poor body image can be associated with depression, anxiety, alcohol and other drug abuse and eating disorders.

Some warning signs that you or someone you know might have body image issues:
- Distorted eating habits
- Obsession with weight and exercise
- Being continually self-critical
- Constantly comparing body size

Guys have body image issues too. One third of males want to be thinner and one third want to be bulkier.

More than **1 in 5** young men say body image is their number one concern.

Tips for better body image:
- Focus on yourself as a person, not just how you look
- Aim to get healthier rather than lose weight
- Focus on the things you like about your body
- Stop being critical about others' appearance
- Remember, real bodies aren't perfect, and perfect bodies are almost always airbrushed.

headspace .org.au/bodyimage
National Youth Mental Health Foundation

From: <https://twitter.com/headspace_aus/status/709546986760851457>. Accessed on: May 15, 2019.

3 Listen to the beginning of a radio interview with actress Karla Mosley. Then mark the correct answers.

   a. Before having an experience with eating disorders, what did she think about them?
   - ○ She thought that only white, rich female adolescents had eating disorders.
   - ○ She thought that eating disorders were the most serious type of mental illness.

   b. What happened to her after having an experience with eating disorders?
   - ○ She realized that it is extremely difficult to be diagnosed with an eating disorder.
   - ○ She realized that anyone can get an eating disorder, regardless of their race.

Karla Mosley

4 Listen to the recording again and take notes on its main ideas. Then complete each sentence with the correct words in parentheses.

   a. Karla Mosley struggled with _____ thoughts about food. (negative/obsessive)

   b. Food haunted her at times; food _____ her at others. (comforted/pleased)

   c. The main causes of her eating disorders were sadness and _____ . (anxiety/low self-esteem)

   d. There was a period in her life when she was throwing up every single _____ . (morning/night)

5 In the beginning of the recording, the radio program host mentions a fact about eating disorders. What is it?

   a. ○ Eating disorders have the highest mortality rate of any psychiatric diagnosis.

   b. ○ Anorexia nervosa has the highest mortality rate of any psychiatric disorder in adolescence.

6 Listen to the recording once more and check your answers.

I WON'T LET A NUMBER ON A SCALE OWN ME.

An Eating Disorder Requires Treatment From

A Doctor A Therapist A Dietitian

Writing

In this unit you have read an advertising poster on page 92, which was part of a campaign about eating disorders. Advertising posters often promote an idea, a campaign, or a product in a visually attractive way. Visit <https://www.nationaleatingdisorders.org/get-involved/nedawareness/resources> to find more advertising posters concerning eating disorders.

- Based on the advertising poster you have read in this unit, create your own advertising poster to invite people to fight against eating disorders.

Follow these instructions to write your text.

1. Think about the target audience (teens, women, people in general) so that you can choose the pictures and the message that best relate to them.
2. Try to get some ideas. Define your slogan or catchy phrase.
3. Below the slogan or catchy phrase, add some relevant information in a smaller font size. Then write a draft of the text.
4. Look for potential images and choose a memorable one that relates to the topic of the text.
5. Place the slogan/catchy phrase, text and images in a visually attractive configuration. Keep your advertising poster attractive.
6. Exchange texts with a classmate and discuss them. Take into consideration the following:
    a. Is the advertising poster suitable for the target audience?
    b. Do the pictures make the text more attractive?
    c. Does the slogan/catchy phrase express the main idea of the text?
7. Make the necessary corrections.
8. Create the final version of your advertising poster. You can use a computer to design it.

It is time to share your advertising poster with your classmates and other people. You can also publish it on the school's website/blog or on a non-profit organization's website. Based on people's reactions to your text, you can continue to improve it.

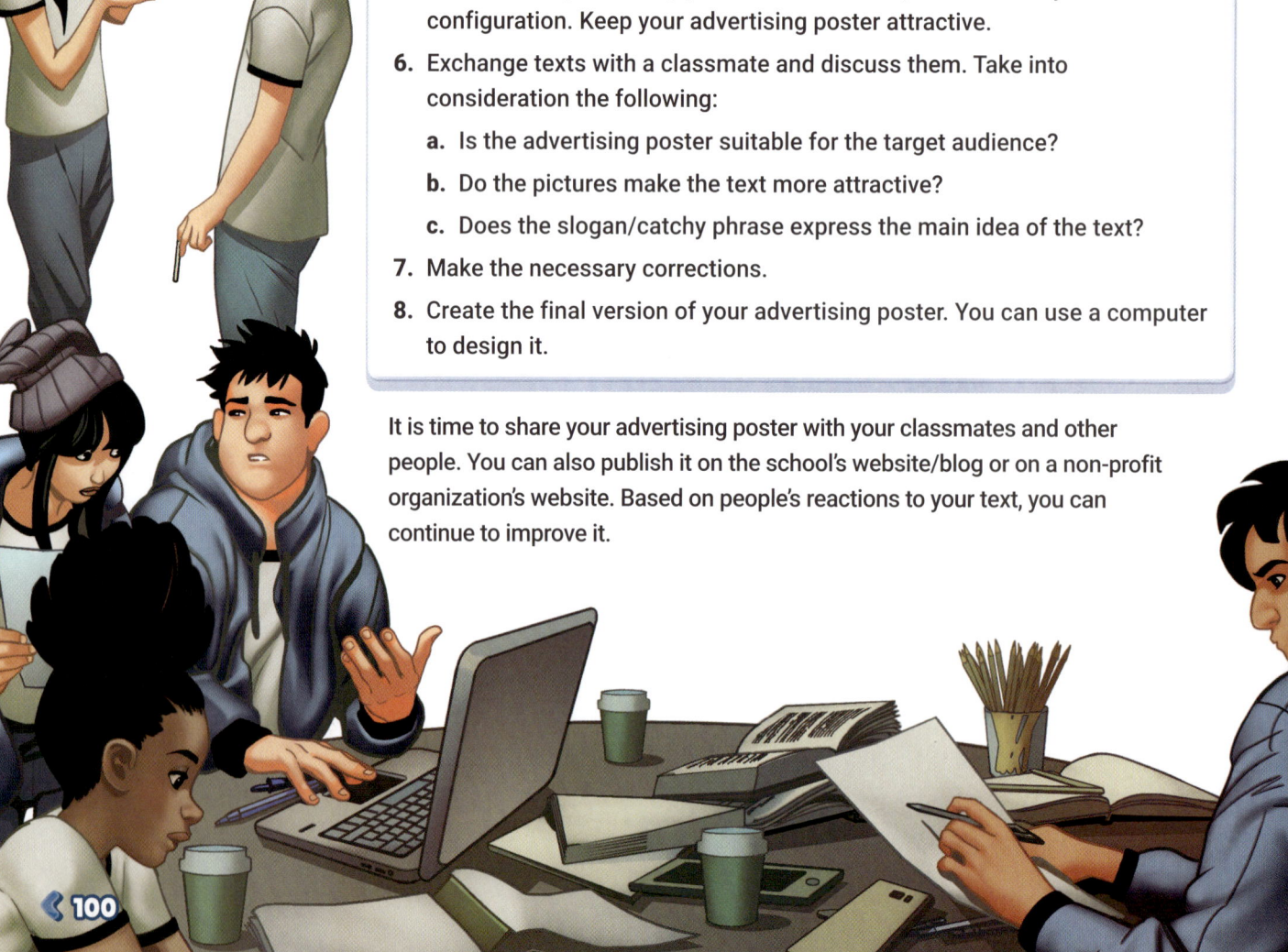

ENGLISH4LIFE

Read this comic strip and do **exercises 1** and **2**.

Comic strip:
- Panel 1: "DIETING IS OVER! WEIGHT LOSS IS OUT!"
- Panel 2: "AMERICANS HAVE FINALLY REJECTED THE IMAGE OF THE SCRAWNY SUPERMODEL AND EMBRACED GOOD NUTRITION AND REGULAR EXERCISE AS THE HEALTHY, HAPPY GOAL OF LIFE!"
- Panel 3: "...EXCEPT THE 17 BILLION PEOPLE WHO SNEAKED OUT AND BOUGHT 'DR. ATKINS' NEW DIET REVOLUTION' LAST WEEK."
- Panel 4: "CHEATERS!! NO ONE CAN BE TRUSTED TO STAY OFF A DIET."

1 Mark the correct answers.

a. Based on the characters' opinion, what should be included in a healthy, happy goal of life?

◯ Dieting and weight loss.   ◯ Good nutrition and regular exercise.

b. What do the 17 billion people mentioned in the text represent?

◯ The ones who want to follow a new diet.

◯ The ones who reject the image of very thin supermodels.

c. What can you infer about "Dr. Atkins' New Diet Revolution"?

◯ It's a book about eating disorders.

◯ It's a bestseller that helps people lose weight.

2 In "Dieting is over!", what does **over** mean?

a. ◯ ended, finished   **b.** ◯ more than a certain amount

3 What does **over** mean in these five sentences? Choose the correct meaning (**I-V**) for each sentence (**a-e**).

a. ◯ Recommended for ages 5 and over.	**I.**	from one side of something to the other side
b. ◯ A huge plane flew over our heads.	**II.**	on the other side of
c. ◯ I climbed over the wall.	**III.**	during a particular period of time
d. ◯ I was in Seattle over the summer.	**IV.**	above or higher than something
e. ◯ The post office is over the bridge.	**V.**	more than an amount, number, or age

From: <https://dictionary.cambridge.org/dictionary/essential-american-english/over_1>. Accessed on: May 15, 2019.

Challenge!

In "Put your things down over here.", what does **over** mean?

✓   ✗

Extra Challenge!

In "I've read the text over and over until I could understand it.", what does **over and over** mean?

✓   ✗

UNIT 8
Rethinking consumerism

Learning Objectives

- to talk about consumerism in modern society;
- to learn vocabulary related to places in town;
- to use the **present perfect** (regular and irregular verbs);
- to explore **quizzes**.

This photo shows people in a Black Friday event in São Paulo. What are they trying to buy? In your opinion, do people often buy things that they don't really need? Are you a conscious shopper? Why (not)?

Getting Started

Places in town

1 Mark the three places where you and your family go shopping most often. What do you usually buy there?

a. ◯ bakery

b. ◯ bookstore

c. ◯ café

d. ◯ clothes store

e. ◯ drugstore/pharmacy

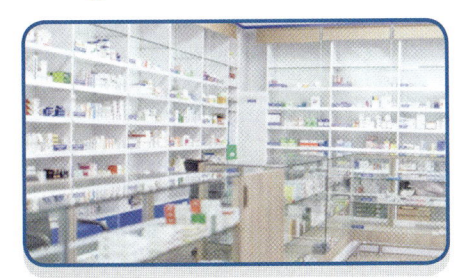

f. ◯ restaurant

g. ◯ shopping mall

h. ◯ supermarket

Language Note

store (US) = shop (UK)

Challenge!

How do you say **bookstore** in BrE?

Extra Challenge!

Which word in AmE is equivalent in meaning to **chemist's** (UK)?

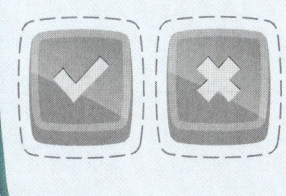

2 Listen to the recording and repeat the words from **exercise 1**.

Reading Comprehension

Pre-Reading

1 Before reading the text, focus on its **title** and **subtitle**. Then, circle the words and expressions you expect to find in the text.

> advertising • antisocial behavior • anxiety • decreased life satisfaction • depression • materialistic tendencies

Reading

2 Read the text below to check your predictions.

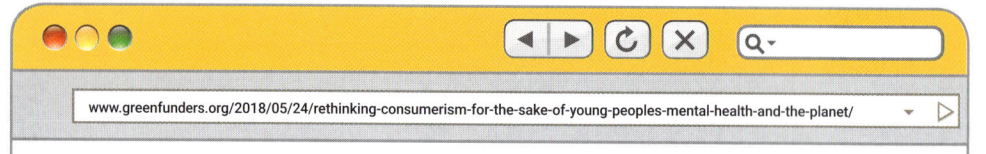

www.greenfunders.org/2018/05/24/rethinking-consumerism-for-the-sake-of-young-peoples-mental-health-and-the-planet/

Rethinking consumerism for the sake of young people's mental health (and the planet)

Consumption and wellbeing

Social scientists have known for years that young people whose 'operating system' aims to accumulate ever more stuff (trainers, houses, jewellery, cars, bags, mobile phones) are less happy than those who prioritise heartier pursuits.

The traits of teens reporting higher wellbeing include spending time with friends and family, hobbies that expand the mind, finding a purpose inside or outside of work, exercising more, spending more time outdoors, and active community involvement.

Buying stuff to meet our needs of course plays an important role in people's lives, but wellbeing studies illustrate that materialistic tendencies are linked to decreased life satisfaction, happiness, vitality and social cooperation, and increases in depression, anxiety, racism and antisocial behaviour.

With young people exposed to more advertising than ever before, including through social media, where their friends and others they follow might be being paid to promote that new jacket they're wearing, shouldn't we be discussing and debating the impacts of consumerism on wellbeing?

According to the Varkey Foundation, British millennials have the second worst mental wellbeing in the world, second only to Japan. Depression rates have doubled in a decade with as many as 24% of girls and 9% of boys aged 14 in the UK experiencing symptoms of depression. One in four young women between the ages of 16 and 24 report having self-harmed and 93% of teachers report increased levels of mental illness in children and young people. Is consumerism partly to blame?

From: <www.greenfunders.org/2018/05/24/rethinking-consumerism-for-the-sake-of-young-peoples-mental-health-and-the-planet/>. Accessed on: May 15, 2019.

Language Note

behaviour (UK) = behavior (US)

jewellery (UK) = jewelry (US)

prioritise (UK) = prioritize (US)

---

heartier = mais substancial

pursuit = busca, procura

trait = característica

On the Web

Consumerism and teens

◂ http://livro.pro/r463gr ▸

(Acesso em: 15 maio 2019).

3 Write **T** (True), **F** (False) or **N** (Not mentioned). Then, correct the false statement(s).

a. ◯ Young people who focus on heartier pursuits are happier than those who accumulate things.

_____

b. ◯ Materialistic tendencies are linked to eating disorders.

_____

c. ◯ Japanese millennials have the second worst mental wellbeing in the world.

_____

4 Read the fragments below and write **F** (Fact) or **O** (Opinion).

a. ◯ "[…] shouldn't we be discussing and debating the impacts of consumerism on wellbeing?"

b. ◯ "[…] 93% of teachers report increased levels of mental illness in children and young people."

5 Write down two examples of activities reported by teens that make them feel healthy and happy.

_____
_____

6 According to the text, "British millennials have the second worst mental wellbeing in the world, second only to Japan." Identify a fragment in the text that shows some evidence for this fact.

_____
_____
_____
_____

Post-Reading

7 Discuss the questions below with a classmate.

a. In your opinion, are there many people who buy stuff just to feel better? What do you think about this behavior? Does what you usually do to feel better contribute to your wellbeing?

b. According to the text, "materialistic tendencies are linked to decreased life satisfaction." In small groups, make a list of three ideas that can be put into practice at your school to discourage materialistic tendencies among teens. Then, share your list with other classmates and get to know different viewpoints on the same topic.

Unit 8 105

Language in Use

Present perfect (regular and irregular verbs)

Read these fragments from the text on page 104 and do **exercises 1** and **2**.

I. "Social scientists **have known** for years that young people […]"

II. "Depression rates **have doubled** in a decade […]"

1 Answer the questions.

a. What time expression is used in fragment **I**?
_____

b. What time expression is used in fragment **II**?
_____

2 Mark the correct answers.

a. Why is the present perfect used in the two fragments?

○ To talk about actions that happened at a specified time in the past.

○ To talk about actions that happened at an unspecified time in the past.

b. Which fragment contains an **irregular verb** in the past participle?

○ Fragment **I** (*known*).

○ Fragment **II** (*doubled*).

income = renda (salário)

3 Read these sentences about consumerism and circle the irregular verbs in the **past participle**. Then, complete the following table.

a. Consumerism has been the topic of considerable discussion over the last decades.

b. Electricity brought westerners an entirely new lifestyle.

c. The increase in resource consumption in richer countries has led to an ever-widening gap between the rich and the poor.

d. Researchers have found that environmental concerns may be pushing some people to buy less.

e. In more recent times, consumer choice has become one of the most common ways for people to engage in issues like sustainability and workers' rights.

BASE FORM	PAST PARTICIPLE
be	
bring	
become	
buy	bought
feel	felt
find	

BASE FORM	PAST PARTICIPLE
keep	kept
have	had
lead	
lose	lost
spend	spent
tell	told

4 Go back to **exercise 3** and notice that there are two sentences with time expressions. Write down the time expressions.

_____

5 Complete this shopping addiction quiz with the verbs in the box as in the example. Use the **past participle**. If necessary, check the list of irregular verbs in **exercise 3**.

bring • buy • feel • have • keep • ~~lose~~ • spend • tell

QUESTIONS	YES	NO
Have you ever _lost_ sight of how much you spent at the mall?	○	○
Has shopping ever _____ problems in your relationships?	○	○
Have you ever _____ remorse after shopping?	○	○
Have you ever _____ money to escape problems?	○	○
Have you _____ your shopping a secret from your friends?	○	○
Have you ever _____ items that you've never even used?	○	○
Have you ever _____ difficulty eating or sleeping because of shopping?	○	○
Have you _____ yourself "this is my last time" and still continued shopping?	○	○

Most compulsive shoppers will answer "yes" to at least four of these questions.

From: <https://mark534183.typeform.com/to/Od8xfO>. Accessed on: May 15, 2019.

6 Now take the quiz and compare your answers with those of a classmate. Are you a compulsive shopper?

Go to **Language Reference** on **page 122**.

Oral Skills

1 What do you know about these three events? Write **I** for **Thanksgiving**, **II** for **Black Friday** or **III** for **Cyber Monday**.

a. ◯ It is a marketing term for the Monday after the Thanksgiving holiday in the United States. It was created by retailers to encourage people to shop online.

b. ◯ It is a holiday celebrated in the U.S., Canada, some of the Caribbean islands, and Liberia. It started as a day of giving thanks for the harvest and the preceding year. It is celebrated on the fourth Thursday of November in the U.S.

c. ◯ It is an informal name for the Friday following Thanksgiving Day in the United States. It has been regarded as the beginning of America's Christmas shopping season since 1952.

2 Listen to the beginning of a radio program and take notes on its main ideas. What event are they talking about?

a. ◯ Thanksgiving in Canada.

b. ◯ Black Friday in Colombia.

c. ◯ Cyber Monday in the United States.

3 Listen to the recording again, take notes and mark the items that are mentioned in it.

a. ◯ Black Friday is when U.S. shoppers take advantage of pre-Christmas discounts.

b. ◯ Black Friday is spreading around the world.

c. ◯ Black Friday began in Colombia two years ago.

d. ◯ Black Friday happens in June and November in Colombia.

e. ◯ There is only one Cyber Monday in Colombia.

4 Listen to the recording once more and check your answers.

5 The English language was used in the recording by two people from different nationalities to communicate with each other. The reporter was from the United States. Where was the person interviewed from?

_____

6 Discuss the questions below with a classmate.

   a. In your opinion, what phenomenon contributes to using English as a language that makes communication possible between people from diverse backgrounds and nationalities? Have you ever seen people from different nationalities use English to talk to each other? If so, describe the experience.

   b. Can you think of different contexts in which people from different nationalities use English for communication?

7 Interview your classmates to find out about their experiences concerning English. Complete the chart below with your classmates' names when their answer is affirmative (e.g. Sure. / Absolutely.). Ask extra questions and take turns as in the example.

FIND SOMEONE WHO...	CLASSMATES' NAMES
has used English outside the school.	
has spoken English with a foreigner.	
has posted a photo caption in English.	
has used English in a trip.	
has traveled to an English-speaking country.	
_____	
_____	

Student A: Have you ever used English outside the school?

Student B: Yeah, once.

Student A: Cool. Where?

Student B: I remember there was this time I was at the mall and two tourists approached me in English.

Different ways of saying 'yes':

Sure.; Totally.; Absolutely.; You bet!; By all means.

Different ways of saying 'no':

Nope.; No way.; Not really.; Not at all.; Not in a million years.

Unit 8

Writing

In this unit you have taken a yes/no quiz on page 107, which was a set of questions designed to evaluate if you are a compulsive shopper. Visit <https://stayteen.org/games/quizzes> and <www.quizony.com/tag-teens.html> to find more examples of quizzes for teens.

- Based on the quiz you have taken in this unit, create your quiz to find out people's experiences concerning shopping.

Follow these instructions to write your text.

1. Choose the subject of the quiz and how many questions you are going to have. Write between five and eight questions.

2. Do research to gather information about the topic chosen (e.g. online shopping, types of shoppers). Look for reliable sources.

3. Check all the pieces of information you get and choose the most relevant ones to write questions about.

4. Write a first draft of the quiz. Include a title for it. You can also include pictures to illustrate your text.

5. Prepare a reference score for the quiz. For example, "Most compulsive shoppers will answer **yes** to at least four of these questions."

6. Exchange quizzes with a classmate and discuss them. Take into consideration the following:

    a. Are the questions clear enough?

    b. Is the information about the topic accurate?

7. Make the necessary corrections.

8. Write the final version of your quiz. You can also use one of the following free services to create an online quiz: <quizyourfriends.com>; <quizzes.cc>.

It is time to share your quiz with your classmates and other people. You can also publish it on the school's website/blog or on a non-profit organization's website. Based on people's reactions to your text, you can continue to improve it.

ENGLISH 4 LIFE

Read this cartoon and do **exercises** 1 and 2.

1 Answer the questions.

a. In your opinion, what is the relationship between the man and the woman?
_____
_____

b. Why is the woman feeling so proud of him?
_____
_____

c. What word does he use to address the woman?
_____

d. What word does she use to address the man?
_____

2 In your opinion, why does the situation portrayed in the cartoon refer to consumerism?
_____
_____

3 **Honey** and **darling** are two examples of informal words used to address a person that is close to you. Use the words in the box to complete the table below.

> babe/baby • gentleman • hon • lady • ma'am • sir • sweetheart • sweetie

POLITE WAYS OF ADDRESSING SOMEONE	INFORMAL WAYS OF ADDRESSING SOMEONE

Always see how others address you and the people around them.

hon = honey

4 Listen to the recording, check your answers and repeat the words.

5 Go back to the table in **exercise 3**. Which polite words are used to address a man and which ones are used to address a woman?
_____

CONSUMERISM FOR BEGINNERS

"LOOK HONEY, I BOUGHT SOMETHING TODAY!"

"OH DARLING, I'M SO PROUD OF YOU!"

Challenge!

Which word do you use before the family name of a woman who is not married, in order to speak/write to her in a polite way?

Extra Challenge!

Which word do you use at the beginning of a letter/email before the name/title of the person you are writing to?

Unit 8

Play 'n' Learn 4

Games

It's time to play a board game with your classmates. Follow the instructions, play 'n' learn!

INSTRUCTIONS

1. Go to START and begin the game by rolling the die.
2. Based on each instruction given, make a sentence in the present perfect to roll the die and move the counter.
3. The player who gets to FINISH first is the winner.

MATERIALS

- a die
- a counter

Board

1. START
2. GO AHEAD 1 SPACE
3. Make a sentence with "increase" in the past participle
4. Make a sentence with "decrease" in the past participle
5. Make a sentence with "start" in the past participle
6. GO BACK 1 SPACE
7. MISS A TURN
8. Make a sentence "Have you ever"
9. Make a sentence with "since"
10. Make a sentence with "since"
11. GO AHEAD 2 SPACES
12. Make a sentence with "for"
13. Make a sentence with "be" in the past participle
14. Make a sentence with "become" in the past participle
15. MISS A TURN

16 ke a sentence "buy" in the past participle

17 GO AHEAD 1 SPACE

18 Make a sentence with "feel" in the past participle

19 Make a sentence with "find" in the past participle

20 MISS A TURN

21 Make a sentence with "keep" in the past participle

22 GO AHEAD 4 SPACES

23 Make a sentence with "have" in the past participle

24 Make a sentence with "lose" in the past participle

25 GO BACK 1 SPACE

26 Make a sentence with "spend" in the past participle

27 Make a sentence with "tell" in the past participle

28 MISS A TURN

29 GO BACK 2 SPACES

30 FINISH

8 AHEAD SPACE

Play 'n' Learn 4

TEST (UNITS 7 AND 8)

1 Circle the time expressions used in these sentences.

   a. The number of eating disorders has increased dramatically over the last decades.

   b. Luckily, she hasn't suffered from any eating disorder since 2016.

   c. Have you seen him lately?

   d. He's recently recovered from bulimia nervosa.

SCORE: _____ / 16 (4 each)

2 Complete the fragments with the correct form of the regular verbs in parentheses. Use the **present perfect**.

> behemoth = monstro

   a. "The average woman sees 400 to 600 advertisements per day, and by the time she is 17 years old, she _____ over 250,000 commercial messages through the media." (receive)

   b. "The number-one wish for girls ages 11 to 17 is to be thinner, and girls as young as five _____ fears of getting fat." (express)

   c. "Eighty percent (80%) of 10-year-old girls _____ , and at any one time, 50% of American women are currently dieting." (diet)

   d. "Adverts for children are a very powerful force. I think we _____ a behemoth we cannot control." (release)

   e. "Increased exposure to images of celebrities' bodies is behind the large rise in the number of young girls being admitted to hospital with an eating disorder, a leading pediatrician _____ ." (claim)

From: <www.healthyplace.com/eating-disorders/articles/eating-disorders-body-image-and-advertising>; <www.theguardian.com/society/2015/jun/25/eating-disorders-rise-children-blamed-celebrity-bodies-advertising>. Accessed on: May 20, 2019.

SCORE: _____ / 25 (5 each)

3 Complete the fragments with the correct form of the irregular verbs in parentheses. Use the **present perfect**.

a. "By treating pre-adolescents as independent, mature consumers, marketers _____ very successful in removing the gatekeepers (parents) from the picture […]." (be)

b. "Teen anger, activism and attitude _____ commodities that marketers co-opt, package and then sell back to teens." (become)

c. "Studies _____ also _____ that boys, like girls, may turn to smoking to help them lose weight." (find)

d. "Advertising _____ always _____ anxiety and it certainly sells anxiety to the young." (sell)

From: <http://mediasmarts.ca/marketing-consumerism/marketing-and-consumerism-special-issues-tweens-and-teens>. Accessed on: May 20, 2019.

SCORE: _____ / 24 (6 each)

4 Complete this text with the correct form of the verbs in parentheses. Use the **present perfect** or the **past simple**.

Raising Minimalist Teenagers In An Age Of Consumerism

Four years ago, we _____ (sell), _____ (donate) or discarded most of our material possessions. It was a decision based on discontent with our current lives. […] We realized we had far too few resources left over for the things most important to us.
Since embarking on this life-giving journey, we _____ (find) this lifestyle resonates effectively with young adults, parents and older generations. But one of our greatest passions is to also inspire teenagers to build a better life by owning less.
For the last 14 years, I _____ (give) my life to teenagers through my full-time employment at nonprofit organizations around the country. I _____ (develop) relationships with hundreds of teens. I _____ (speak) at public schools and student conferences. I _____ (write) books for teenagers. In short, I love the opportunity to invest in their lives and introduce them to a better way to live. […]

From: <https://goodmenproject.com/families/raising-minimalist-teenagers-in-an-age-of-consumerism-admc/>. Accessed on: May 20, 2019.

SCORE: _____ / 35 (5 each)   **TOTAL:** _____ / 100

Go to **My Achievements** on **page 117**.

Project

TASK

In small groups, create an ad that encourages people to be proud of their shapes and colors. The aim of the campaign is to create positive body image by raising people's awareness of body acceptance. Use a persuasive tone in your ad by choosing a strong slogan or headline message (e.g. "I am unique.", "My body, my rules.", "You are beautiful the way you are."). Don't forget to choose a memorable picture or make a drawing to illustrate it. Then share all the ads among teachers, family members, friends and other people from your community.

An example:

I WANT TO INSPIRE PEOPLE.
I WANT SOMEONE TO LOOK AT ME AND SAY "BECAUSE OF YOU I DIDN'T GIVE UP"

LOVE AUTHENTIC

From: <www.loveauthentic.co.za/blog/alvina-motilall-my-vitiligo-campaign>. Accessed on: May 20, 2019.

Evaluating

Answer the questions below to evaluate the development of the project.

a. What have you learned from the project?

b. Did you have any difficulties? If so, what helped you overcome them?

c. Would you do anything differently? If so, what? Why?

My Achievements

Go back to **Unit 7** and **Unit 8** and check how many ticks (✓) you have. Use the table below to help you count the total number of ticks.

UNIT 7	CHALLENGE!	EXTRA CHALLENGE!
page 93		
page 101		
UNIT 8	**CHALLENGE!**	**EXTRA CHALLENGE!**
page 103		
page 111		

TOTAL NUMBER OF TICKS: _____ /8

Check what you get:

▶ **1 - 2 ticks** = 1 sticker (a weather app)

▶ **3 - 5 ticks** = 2 stickers (a weather app and a maps app)

▶ **6 - 8 ticks** = 3 stickers (a weather app, a maps app and a calendar app)

Find your stickers in the **Stickers** section and place them on page 144.

Based on your total score in **Test (Units 7 and 8)**, see what you get:

▶ **60 to 79** = a bronze medal sticker

▶ **80 to 89** = a silver medal sticker

▶ **90 to 100** = a golden medal sticker

Find your sticker in the **Stickers** section and place it here.

PLACE YOUR STICKER HERE.

How do you feel about your **commitment** and **participation** in classes? Consider the development of the four skills (reading, writing, listening and speaking).

Find your sticker in the **Stickers** section and place it above.

Play 'n' Learn 4

Language Reference

UNIT 1

Review: Word formation (prefixes and suffixes)

Leia o fragmento a seguir e observe o uso do prefixo **un-** em *uncomfortable* e *unsafe* e o uso dos sufixos **-able** em *uncomfortable* e **-ly** em *immediately*.

> "If you see something online that makes you feel uncomfortable, unsafe or worried: leave the website, turn off your computer if you want to and tell a trusted adult immediately."

From: <www.safetynetkids.org.uk/personal-safety/staying-safe-online/>. Accessed on: May 20, 2019.

No texto acima, o prefixo **un-** foi acrescentado aos adjetivos *comfortable* e *safe* para formar, respectivamente, os adjetivos *uncomfortable* e *unsafe*, que têm significados opostos aos dos adjetivos iniciais. O acréscimo de prefixos altera o significado das palavras, mas, em geral, não muda sua classe gramatical. O acréscimo de sufixos, no entanto, geralmente altera a classe gramatical da palavra (o substantivo *comfort*, ao receber o sufixo **-able**, formou o adjetivo *(un)comfortable*, e o adjetivo *immediate*, ao receber o sufixo **-ly**, formou o advérbio *immediately*). A seguir, observe alguns exemplos de palavras formadas por prefixos e/ou sufixos.

Don't be unkind or aggressive on the Internet.
Be careful who you give your number to.

Veja, nos quadros a seguir, palavras formadas por prefixos e sufixos que apareceram ao longo da **unidade 1**, **Play 'n' Learn 1** e **Workbook (Unit 1)**.

PREFIXES	EXAMPLES	MEANING
in-	inappropriate, indecipherable, inoffensive	not
un-	unauthorized, uncomfortable, unhappy, unkind, unsafe, unsecured, unsuitable	

SUFFIXES	EXAMPLES	MEANING
-able	indecipherable, uncomfortable	able to
-al	personal	related to
-ful	careful, thoughtful	full of
-ly	automatically, carefully, easily, extremely, regularly, safely, securely, typically	in a particular way
-ship	friendship	state or condition of
-tion	connection, information, location, manipulation	process or state of

UNIT 2

Linking words/phrases

Leia a tirinha a seguir e observe o uso do conector **if**.

Na tirinha, utilizou-se o conector **if** para introduzir uma condição, no caso, uma situação hipotética ("se essas paredes pudessem falar"). Conectores (*linking words/phrases*) são palavras empregadas para ligar, conectar duas ou mais palavras, frases, orações e parágrafos.

Veja, no quadro a seguir, alguns conectores que foram utilizados ao longo deste livro e as ideias expressas por eles.

	EXAMPLES
Addition	and, also, as well as, besides, in addition, moreover, not only… but also, too
Cause	as, because, due to
Comparison	as, like
Condition	except if, if, unless
Contrast	but, however, whereas, while
Exemplification	for example, for instance, like, such as
Purpose	in order to, so that, to
Result	as a result, so
Sequence	after (that), before (that), finally, first(ly), then

UNIT 3

First conditional

Leia o fragmento a seguir e observe o uso da oração condicional do tipo 1 (*first conditional*).

"If you rub two balloons on a sweater, and hang them from strings, the balloons will repel each other. Why? Because they are both negatively charged. Similar charges repel."

From: <https://bpsscience.weebly.com/uploads/2/2/1/3/2213712/4_making_static_magnetism__electricity__grade_4.pdf>. Accessed on: May 20, 2019.

No texto, utilizou-se a oração condicional do tipo 1 para apresentar uma situação que pode acontecer no futuro ("Se você esfregar dois balões em um suéter e pendurá-los com cordas, eles irão se repelir"). A seguir, observe alguns exemplos de frases com orações condicionais do tipo 1.

If I see her, *I will talk to her*.

I won't go to the beach **if it rains**.

Veja, no quadro a seguir, a estrutura da oração condicional do tipo 1.

If + verbo principal no *present simple*	,	*will* + forma básica do verbo principal
will + forma básica do verbo principal		*if* + verbo principal no *present simple*

Language Reference

UNIT 4

Second conditional

Leia o fragmento a seguir e observe o uso das duas orações condicionais do tipo 2 (*second conditional*).

> "**The thought experiment: What would happen if the Earth stopped spinning?**
>
> If Earth stopped rotating and fell to a standstill, humanity would be in trouble."
>
> From: <www.sciencefocus.com/planet-earth/the-thought-experiment-what-would-happen-if-the-earth-stopped-spinning/>. Accessed on: May 20, 2019.

No texto, foram utilizadas duas orações condicionais do tipo 2 para apresentar situações improváveis de acontecer ("o que aconteceria se a Terra parasse de girar?" e "... a humanidade estaria em apuros"). A seguir, observe alguns exemplos de frases com orações condicionais do tipo 2.

If I were an animal, I would be a dog.

I could help you *if you trusted me*.

Veja, no quadro a seguir, a estrutura da oração condicional do tipo 2.

If + verbo principal no *past simple*	would/could + forma básica do verbo principal
would/could + forma básica do verbo principal	if + verbo principal no *past simple*

Em orações condicionais do tipo 2, geralmente usamos a forma do verbo *to be* no modo subjuntivo (*If I were you*).

If I were you, I would do everything completely different.

UNIT 5

Modal verbs: may/might

Leia a tirinha a seguir e observe o uso do verbo modal *might*.

Na tirinha, utilizou-se o verbo modal *might* para expressar uma possibilidade, no caso, a possibilidade de estar na hora de Jon limpar a geladeira. Usamos, geralmente, *might* e *may* para indicar possibilidade, conforme os exemplos a seguir.

Jon **may** be wrong.

Jon believes it **might** be time to clean the refrigerator.

A partir dos exemplos anteriores, veja que os verbos modais são utilizados antes da forma básica do verbo principal (*may be*, *might be*). Em frases na forma negativa, utiliza-se *not* entre o verbo modal e o verbo principal.

Jon **may not** be right.

Garfield **might not** agree with Jon.

UNIT 6

Modal verbs: should/must/have to

Leia a tirinha a seguir e observe o uso do verbo modal *should*.

Na tirinha, utilizou-se o verbo modal *should* para fazer uma recomendação a si próprio ("ir mais devagar, no seu tempo"). Veja que os verbos modais são utilizados antes da forma básica do verbo principal (*should slow down*). Em frases na forma negativa, utiliza-se *not* entre o verbo modal e o verbo principal.

*Garfield **should** relax more.*

*Garfield **should not** be agitated.*

Veja, no quadro a seguir, outros verbos modais e, a partir dos exemplos de uso, identifique as ideias expressas por eles.

MODAL VERBS	EXAMPLES	MEANINGS
should/ shouldn't	Helping others **should** be fun. Helping others **shouldn't** be boring.	aconselhamento, recomendação
have to/ must	You **have to** respect everybody. You **must** respect everybody.	necessidade, obrigatoriedade
not have to	You **don't have to** work every day.	ausência de necessidade ou obrigatoriedade
mustn't	You **mustn't** break the law.	proibição

mustn't = must not
shouldn't = should not

UNIT 7

Present perfect (regular verbs)

Leia o fragmento a seguir e observe o uso do *present perfect*.

"Over the last four decades, the reported prevalence of eating disorders has increased, although there is no indication as to whether this is due to more awareness of the problem or more people experiencing eating disorders. Beat estimates that there are more than 1.25m people with an eating disorder across the UK."

From: <www.theguardian.com/society/2019/feb/15/hospital-admissions-for-eating-disorders-surge-to-highest-in-eight-years>. Accessed on: May 20, 2019.

No texto, utilizou-se o *present perfect* para dizer que a prevalência reportada de transtornos alimentares tem aumentado nas últimas quatro décadas (*Over the last four decades, the reported prevalence of eating disorders has increased*). Veja que o verbo principal é regular (*increased*). É comum utilizarmos o *present perfect* para falarmos de ações que começaram no passado e continuam no presente, conforme os exemplos a seguir.

Language Reference

Anorexia among girls **has increased** a lot over the last decades.

Recently, many teenagers **have developed** eating disorders.

Veja, nos quadros a seguir, as formas **afirmativa**, **negativa**, **interrogativa** e as **respostas curtas** do *present perfect*.

AFFIRMATIVE FORM

I / You / We / You / They	have	changed	lately.
He / She / It	has		

NEGATIVE FORM

I / You / We / You / They	haven't	changed	lately.
He / She / It	hasn't		

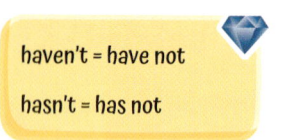

haven't = have not
hasn't = has not

INTERROGATIVE FORM

Have	I / you / we / you / they	changed	lately?
Has	he / she / it		

SHORT ANSWERS

Yes,	I / you / we / you / they	have.
	he / she / it	has.

SHORT ANSWERS

No,	I / you / we / you / they	haven't.
	he / she / it	hasn't.

A palavra **ever** é geralmente utilizada em frases no *present perfect* para fazer referência a alguma vez que determinada ação aconteceu.

Have you **ever** suffered from an eating disorder?

Has advertising **ever** influenced you?

A palavra **since** é geralmente utilizada em frases no *present perfect* para dizer quando uma ação foi iniciada. Já a palavra **for** introduz o período de tempo de uma ação.

They've lived here **since** 2008.

They've lived here **for** over ten years.

UNIT 8

Present perfect (irregular verbs)

Veja, no quadro a seguir, os principais **verbos irregulares no passado e particípio passado** organizados por ordem alfabética.

FORMA BÁSICA	PASSADO	PARTICÍPIO PASSADO	TRADUÇÃO*
be	was, were	been	ser, estar
bear	bore	borne	suportar, ser portador de
beat	beat	beaten	bater
become	became	become	tornar-se
begin	began	begun	começar
behold	beheld	beheld	contemplar
bend	bent	bent	curvar
bet	bet	bet	apostar
bid	bid	bid	oferecer, fazer uma oferta
bind	bound	bound	unir, vincular, comprometer
bite	bit	bitten	morder
bleed	bled	bled	sangrar, ter hemorragia

FORMA BÁSICA	PASSADO	PARTICÍPIO PASSADO	TRADUÇÃO*
blow	blew	blown	assoprar, explodir
break	broke	broken	quebrar
breed	bred	bred	procriar, reproduzir
bring	brought	brought	trazer
broadcast	broadcast	broadcast	transmitir, irradiar
build	built	built	construir
burn	burnt/burned	burnt/burned	queimar
buy	bought	bought	comprar
catch	caught	caught	pegar, capturar
choose	chose	chosen	escolher
come	came	come	vir
cost	cost	cost	custar
cut	cut	cut	cortar
deal	dealt	dealt	negociar, tratar
dig	dug	dug	cavar, escavar
do	did	done	fazer
draw	drew	drawn	desenhar
dream	dreamt/dreamed	dreamt/dreamed	sonhar
drink	drank	drunk	beber
drive	drove	driven	dirigir, ir de carro
eat	ate	eaten	comer
fall	fell	fallen	cair
feed	fed	fed	alimentar
feel	felt	felt	sentir(-se)
fight	fought	fought	lutar
find	found	found	achar, encontrar

FORMA BÁSICA	PASSADO	PARTICÍPIO PASSADO	TRADUÇÃO*
flee	fled	fled	fugir, escapar
fly	flew	flown	voar, pilotar
forbid	forbade	forbidden	proibir
forget	forgot	forgotten	esquecer
forgive	forgave	forgiven	perdoar
freeze	froze	frozen	congelar, paralisar
get	got	got/gotten	obter
give	gave	given	dar
go	went	gone	ir
grow	grew	grown	crescer, cultivar
hang	hung	hung	pendurar
have	had	had	ter, beber, comer
hear	heard	heard	ouvir
hide	hid	hidden/hid	esconder
hit	hit	hit	bater
hold	held	held	segurar
hurt	hurt	hurt	machucar
keep	kept	kept	guardar, manter
know	knew	known	saber, conhecer
lay	laid	laid	colocar em posição horizontal, assentar
lead	led	led	liderar
learn	learnt/learned	learnt/learned	aprender
leave	left	left	deixar, partir
lend	lent	lent	emprestar (dar emprestado)

Language Reference

FORMA BÁSICA	PASSADO	PARTICÍPIO PASSADO	TRADUÇÃO*
let	let	let	deixar, alugar
lie	lay	lain	deitar
lose	lost	lost	perder, extraviar
make	made	made	fazer, fabricar
mean	meant	meant	significar, querer dizer
meet	met	met	encontrar, conhecer
overcome	overcame	overcome	superar
overtake	overtook	overtaken	alcançar, surpreender
pay	paid	paid	pagar
put	put	put	colocar
quit	quit	quit	deixar, abandonar
read	read	read	ler
ride	rode	ridden	andar de (bicicleta etc.), andar a (cavalo)
ring	rang	rung	tocar (campainha, sinos etc.)
rise	rose	risen	subir, erguer-se
run	ran	run	correr, concorrer, dirigir
say	said	said	dizer
see	saw	seen	ver
seek	sought	sought	procurar obter, objetivar
sell	sold	sold	vender
send	sent	sent	mandar

FORMA BÁSICA	PASSADO	PARTICÍPIO PASSADO	TRADUÇÃO*
set	set	set	estabelecer, colocar, pôr em determinada condição, marcar, ajustar
shake	shook	shaken	sacudir, tremer
shine	shone	shone	brilhar
shoot	shot	shot	atirar, alvejar
shrink	shrank	shrunk	encolher, contrair
shut	shut	shut	fechar, cerrar
sing	sang	sung	cantar
sink	sank	sunk	afundar, submergir
sit	sat	sat	sentar
sleep	slept	slept	dormir
slide	slid	slid	deslizar, escorregar
smell	smelled/smelt	smelled/smelt	cheirar
speak	spoke	spoken	falar
spend	spent	spent	gastar
spin	spun	spun	girar, fiar
spit	spit/spat	spit/spat	cuspir
spread	spread	spread	espalhar
stand	stood	stood	parar de pé, aguentar
steal	stole	stolen	roubar
stick	stuck	stuck	furar, fincar, enfiar
stink	stank	stunk	cheirar mal
strike	struck	struck	golpear, desferir, atacar

FORMA BÁSICA	PASSADO	PARTICÍPIO PASSADO	TRADUÇÃO*
strive	strove	striven	esforçar-se, lutar
swear	swore	sworn	jurar, prometer, assegurar
sweep	swept	swept	varrer
swim	swam	swum	nadar
swing	swung	swung	balançar, alternar
take	took	taken	tomar
teach	taught	taught	ensinar, dar aula
tear	tore	torn	rasgar, despedaçar
tell	told	told	contar, dizer
think	thought	thought	pensar
throw	threw	thrown	atirar, arremessar
undergo	underwent	undergone	submeter-se a, suportar
understand	understood	understood	entender
uphold	upheld	upheld	sustentar, apoiar, defender
wear	wore	worn	vestir, usar, gastar (pelo uso)
weep	wept	wept	chorar
win	won	won	vencer, ganhar
write	wrote	written	escrever, redigir

* Apresentamos aqui os sentidos mais comuns dos verbos listados.

Veja, nos quadros a seguir, os principais **verbos irregulares no passado e particípio passado agrupados por formas semelhantes**. Em seguida, ouça o áudio referente a cada grupo e perceba as semelhanças na pronúncia dos verbos.

22 A. Passado com o som /an/ /aŋ/ e particípio passado com o som /ʌn/ /ʌŋ/

FORMA BÁSICA	PASSADO	PARTICÍPIO PASSADO	TRADUÇÃO
begin	began	begun	começar
drink	drank	drunk	beber
ring	rang	rung	tocar (campainha, sinos, telefone etc.)
run	ran	run	correr, concorrer; dirigir
shrink	shrank	shrunk	encolher, contrair
sing	sang	sung	cantar
sink	sank	sunk	afundar, submergir
stink	stank	stunk	cheirar mal
swim	swam	swum	nadar

23 B. Passado com o som /əʊ/ e particípio passado com o som /əʊ/ terminado em *en*

FORMA BÁSICA	PASSADO	PARTICÍPIO PASSADO	TRADUÇÃO
break	broke	broken	quebrar
choose	chose	chosen	escolher
freeze	froze	frozen	congelar, paralisar
speak	spoke	spoken	falar
steal	stole	stolen	roubar

24 C. Passado e particípio passado com o som /ɔ:t/

FORMA BÁSICA	PASSADO	PARTICÍPIO PASSADO	TRADUÇÃO
bring	brought	brought	trazer
buy	bought	bought	comprar
catch	caught	caught	pegar, capturar
fight	fought	fought	lutar
seek	sought	sought	procurar, obter, objetivar
teach	taught	taught	ensinar, dar aula
think	thought	thought	pensar

25 D. Passado com o som /u:/ e particípio passado com o som /əʊn/

FORMA BÁSICA	PASSADO	PARTICÍPIO PASSADO	TRADUÇÃO
blow	blew	blown	assoprar, explodir
draw	drew	drawn	desenhar
fly	flew	flown	voar, pilotar
grow	grew	grown	crescer, cultivar
know	knew	known	saber, conhecer
throw	threw	thrown	atirar, arremessar

26 E. Passado e particípio passado com o som /ɛnt/

FORMA BÁSICA	PASSADO	PARTICÍPIO PASSADO	TRADUÇÃO
bend	bent	bent	curvar
lend	lent	lent	dar emprestado
send	sent	sent	mandar
spend	spent	spent	gastar

27 F. Passado e particípio passado com o som /ept/

FORMA BÁSICA	PASSADO	PARTICÍPIO PASSADO	TRADUÇÃO
keep	kept	kept	guardar, manter
sleep	slept	slept	dormir
sweep	swept	swept	varrer
weep	wept	wept	chorar

Workbook

UNIT 1

1 What do these chat abbreviations stand for?

a. BRB _____

b. BTW _____

c. F2F _____

d. FYI _____

e. XOXOXO _____

f. IDK _____

g. LOL _____

h. THX/THNX _____

2 Complete the sentences with the words in parentheses and an appropriate **prefix** or **suffix**.

a. Don't be _____ or aggressive online. (kind)

b. Be _____ who you give your number to. (care)

c. People _____ post happy photos and stories on the Internet. (typical)

d. People don't usually share their _____ moments on the Internet. (happy)

e. Pick a password you can _____ remember but no one else can guess. (easy)

f. Talk to an adult if someone makes you feel _____ online. (comfort)

g. Flattering messages may be more about _____ than _____ . (manipulate/friend)

> flattering = elogioso(a)

UNIT 2

1 How are these people feeling?

a. _____

b. _____

c. _____

d. _____

e. _____ f. _____

2 Complete the sentences with the linking words/phrases from the box.

> for instance • not only... but also • like • whereas

a. We convey emotions through different mechanisms, such as facial expressions and gestures.

We convey emotions through different mechanisms, _____ .

b. You can easily fake positive emotions, but negative emotions are very difficult to fake.

You can easily fake positive emotions, _____ .

c. Different colors spark different emotions in us. For example, blue helps to calm down a person.

Different colors spark different emotions in us. _____ .

d. People experience emotions when they are awake and also when they are dreaming.

People experience emotions _____ .

> spark = provocar, despertar

3 Focus on the interjections in **bold** and infer how people are feeling. Match the columns.

a. We won the game. **Yay!**   ◯ sorry

b. **Oops!** I forgot your birthday.   ◯ surprised

c. **Ugh**, I'm not going to eat this!   ◯ relieved

d. **Wow!** What a beautiful living room.   ◯ excited

e. I'm so glad everything went well. **Phew!**   ◯ disgusted

UNIT 3

1 Complete the sentences with **do** or **find**.

a. Next class we're going to _____ a science experiment.

b. Scientists are trying to _____ an answer to that question.

c. _____ some research immediately. Do you understand?

d. People should _____ some time for reading every day.

2 Use the **first conditional** to complete the sentences.

a. If the science teacher _____ (help) us, we'll finish the experiment.

b. If you are prepared, you _____ (pass) the test.

c. I _____ (not go) to the park if it rains.

d. If I see him, I _____ (talk) to him.

3 Put the words into the correct order to write sentences.

a. they're / If / they'll / free, / come.

_____
_____

b. miss / you / If / hurry, / bus. / don't / the / you'll

_____
_____

c. if / go / more sustainable / by bike. / will / to / It / school / be / you

_____

Workbook 129

UNIT 4

1 Complete the sentences with the expressions from the box.

> spare time • make time • right on time • take your time • waste time

a. She writes poetry in her _____ .

b. I don't want to _____ arguing with you!

c. For the first time I wasn't late. I got there _____.

d. We don't need the results now. You can _____.

e. They're always so busy that it is difficult for them to _____ for the kids.

2 Use the **second conditional** to complete the quotes.

a. "I _____ (work) every day if I could." – Jean Nidetch

b. "If it were not for hopes, the heart _____ (break)." – Thomas Fuller

c. "If I were an animal, I _____ (be) an eagle." – Jamie Foxx

d. "If I _____ (have) to choose, I would rather have birds than airplanes." – Charles Lindbergh

> From: <www.latimes.com/archives/la-xpm-1988-01-21-vw-37478-story.html>; DEMAKIS, Joseph M. The ultimate book of quotations. Raleigh: Lulu Enterprises, 2012. p. 202>; <www.lawattstimes.com/index.php?option=com_content&view=article&id=751:jamie-unchained-jamie-foxx-the-django-unchained-interview&catid=27&Itemid=117>; <http://movies2.nytimes.com/books/98/09/27/specials/lindbergh-conservationist.html>. Accessed on: May 20, 2019.

3 Put the words into the correct order to write sentences.

a. you / trusted / If / I / help / me, / you. / could

_____

_____

b. if / English / every day. / practiced / You / could / you / learn / it / faster

_____

_____

c. lottery? / would / if / What / won / the / you / do / you

_____

_____

UNIT 5

1 Solve the word search below and find **10 Internet-related words**.

P	O	D	C	A	S	T	X	Q	C
H	E	A	O	E	D	G	Q	K	S
M	H	L	A	M	V	I	V	Q	P
R	Q	I	G	A	I	X	S	Y	A
J	O	N	L	I	N	E	A	F	M
U	T	K	J	L	B	W	W	C	D
B	G	C	V	L	O	G	X	H	G
L	U	X	P	M	X	W	T	A	V
O	E	L	N	T	A	S	M	T	B
G	I	G	F	A	Q	L	E	S	B

2 Complete these headlines with the words from the box.

> may be • may reveal • might not expect • might not be

a. "Finland is winning the war on fake news. What it's learned _____ crucial to Western democracy"

From: <https://edition.cnn.com/interactive/2019/05/europe/finland-fake-news-intl/>. Accessed on: May 20, 2019.

b. "Massive study of fake news _____ why it spreads so easily

Fake news thrives for reasons you _____ ."

From: <https://futurism.com/fake-news-study-spread>. Accessed on: May 20, 2019.

c. "Why fighting fake news with the facts _____ enough"

From: <www.nytimes.com/2019/01/09/books/review-misinformation-age-cailin-oconnor-james-owen-weatherall-down-to-earth-bruno-latour.html>. Accessed on: May 20, 2019.

UNIT 6

1 Match the columns.

a. You **should** stay here. ○ It means *you have to stay here*.

b. You **must** stay here. ○ It means *you don't need to stay here*.

c. You **mustn't** stay here. ○ It means *you are advised to stay here*.

d. You **don't have to** stay here. ○ It means *you are prohibited from staying here*.

2 Complete the text with the correct modal verbs in parentheses.

[...]

Volunteer work will help teach you skills that can be immediately applied in the workplace. When volunteering, you can build collaborative skills. Sure you can learn team work with group projects in school, but you'll learn much more building a house with people you just met with an organization like Habitat for Humanity,

or you _____ (might/should) learn customer service skills when handing out food for people at a local soup kitchen or Community Gardens of Tucson. Teamwork and customer service will also help you build more confidence when speaking with others if you're shy.

[...]

Builds Networking Skills

By volunteering, you'll meet new people from different backgrounds and make friends that you _____ (might not/must not) have expected to make. You're also building connections with organizations that _____ (might/must) lead to a job or a recommendation for hire. The people you meet can also be references on your resume. When volunteering don't forget the real reason that you are giving back, it _____ (should/shouldn't) only be to benefit yourself but to help others, make a difference and make new friends!

Helps Find Your Passion

When considering volunteer opportunities, you _____ (should/don't have to) start with ones that interest you. By volunteering at a museum, hospital, or animal shelter you can learn what it's like to work in those certain fields. This is a great way to learn what you like and don't like before you even get an actual job. [...]

From: <www.hughesfcu.org/blog/detail/2018/05/16/4-reasons-teens-should-volunteer-now!>. Accessed on: May 20, 2019.

resume = currículo

UNIT 7

1 Circle the time expressions used in these sentences.

a. He's **recently** launched a campaign for body acceptance.

b. Online advertising has increased dramatically **since 2016**.

c. He's been in the marketing industry **over the last years**.

d. **Lately**, I've suffered from insomnia.

2 Complete the fragments with the correct form of the regular verbs in parentheses. Use the **present perfect**.

a. "In fact, 51% of smartphone users _____ a new company or product when searching on their smartphones." (discover)

b. "Video ad completion rates _____ steadily _____ over the past few years, reaching 70% overall in 2017." (increase)

c. "As an internet user, you're likely among the majority that dislikes pop-up ads. In fact, 81% of consumers _____ a browser or exited a webpage because of one [...]." (close)

d. "While many marketers focused their attention on the potential uses of virtual reality (VR) over the past few years, that attention _____ now _____ to augmented reality (AR)." (shift)

From: <www.wordstream.com/blog/ws/2018/07/19/advertising-statistics>. Accessed on: May 20, 2019.

shift = mudar
steadily = continuamente

UNIT 8

1 Complete the fragments with the correct form of the irregular verbs in parentheses. Use the **present perfect**.

a. "Football and consumerism seem to _____ intertwined, and the same thing is happening in many other sports [...]." (become)

b. "Modern advertising [...] is now about creating wants and needs that we might not _____ _____ before seeing the advertisement." (have)

c. "As we _____, consumerism is an idea that is woven into the fabric of our modern society." (see)

d. "[...] the modern form of consumerism _____ way too far and is taking our lives, hopes and happiness with it." (go)

From: <www.lifesquared.org.uk/problem-consumerism>. Accessed on: May 20, 2019.

> fabric = tecido, pano
>
> intertwine = entrelaçado(a), interligado(a)
>
> woven = tecido(a), trançado(a)

2 Complete each sentence with the appropriate word in parentheses.

a. What's up, _____? (dude/sir)

b. Are you ready to order, _____? (dude/sir)

c. Excuse me, _____. Would you mind showing me the way to the post office? (ma'am/sweetie)

d. _____, can you carry this bag for me? (Ma'am/Sweetie)

Glossary

A

a few: alguns, algumas
abound: abundar, existir em abundância
account: conta
accurate: preciso(a)
addict: viciado(a)
addiction: vício
address: abordar, dirigir-se a
advertising: propaganda
against: contra
allow: permitir
amount: quantidade
anger: raiva
angry: zangado(a)

annoy: aborrecer
annoyed: aborrecido(a)
anywhere: qualquer lugar
approach: abordar, aproximar-se
arrow: seta

aspire: aspirar, ambicionar
at least: pelo menos
available: disponível
avoid: evitar
awake: acordado(a)
awarded: premiado(a)
awareness: consciência

B

bake sale: venda de assados caseiros (bolos, pães etc.) para arrecadação de fundos para caridade ou evento especial
beard: barba
beauty: beleza
behavior: comportamento
belief: crença
bet: apostar
bit: pedaço
blame: culpar
blood: sangue
blood vessel: vaso sanguíneo

bored: entediado(a)
boring: entediante
both: ambos(as)

brain: cérebro

bring: trazer

broaden: alargar

bulkier: mais corpulento

busy: ocupado(a)

by the way: a propósito

C

caption: legenda

care about: preocupar-se, importar-se

carrier: portador

catch: pegar, capturar

catchy: atraente

challenging: desafiador(a)

change: mudar; mudança

charged: carregado(a)

cheater: traidor

chore: tarefa

claim: afirmar, alegar, reivindicar; reivindicação

climb: subir, escalar

comb: pente; pentear

come up with: encontrar; sugerir, inventar

commitment: compromisso

committed: comprometido(a)

comprehensive: abrangente

concerned: preocupado(a)

concur: concordar

confidence: confiança

convey: transmitir

counseling: aconselhamento

countless: incontável

credible: confiável

cut off: cortar, suspender

D

dangerous: perigoso(a)

deceptively: enganosamente

decipher: decifrar

decreased: diminuído(a), reduzido(a)

deed: feito

deliberately: deliberadamente

delight: prazer, alegria

demand: exigir

desire: desejo

develop: desenvolver

developing: em desenvolvimento

device: dispositivo

dilation: dilatação

dirt: sujeira, terra

discourage: desencorajar

discovery: descoberta

disease: doença

disgust: nojo, repugnância

disgusted: enojado(a)

double: dobrar; dobro

doubt: dúvida

dozen: dúzia

draft: rascunho

drag: arrastar

drive: impulso

drop: soltar

dubious: duvidoso(a)

due to: devido a

dysmorphia: dismorfia

E

eagle: águia

earlier: mais cedo

embrace: abraçar

employer: empregador

enough: suficiente

ensure: assegurar

envy: inveja

ever-widening: alargamento crescente

evolve: evoluir, desenvolver-se

expensive: caro(a)

F

fabrication: falsidade, mentira

fail: fracassar

fake: falso(a); fingir, simular; falsificação

fear: medo

feature: característica

feeling: sentimento

few: pouco(s)/pouca(s)

field: campo, área

fight: lutar

figure out: compreender

find: encontrar, achar

finding: achado, resultado

fire: fogo

firefighter: bombeiro(a)

fit: enquadrar-se, encaixar

flood: inundação

flowchart: fluxograma

fool: enganar

foolish: idiota, bobo

for the sake of: por uma questão de

foreigner: estrangeiro(a)

forget: esquecer

fuel: combustível

G

gap: lacuna

gatekeeper: guardião/guardiã

gather: coletar, juntar

graceful: gracioso(a)

grateful: grato(a)

great aunt: tia-avó

great uncle: tio-avô

guest: convidado(a)

guy: cara

H

hands-on: prático(a)

hang out: passar tempo ocioso com alguém

harmful: prejudicial

harvest: colheita

haunt: assombrar

headache: dor de cabeça

health: saúde

healthy: sadio; saudável

hear: ouvir

heart: coração

heavy: pesado

height: altura

high: alto

highs and lows: altos e baixos

highlight: destacar

homeless: sem teto, sem moradia

hope: esperar

hopefully: esperançosamente

host: apresentador

hotspot: ponto de acesso

hug: abraço

huge: enorme

I

illness: doença

increase: aumentar

increasingly: cada vez mais, de forma crescente

indecipherable: indecifrável

indulge: deixar-se levar

issue: assunto, questão, problema

J

joy: alegria

joyful: alegre

K

kind: gentil

kindness: gentileza

L

laugh: rir

launch: lançar

lead: conduzir, levar

leave: partir

less: menos

lifetime: período de vida

likely: provável

literacy: letramento

little: pouco

long-term: de longo prazo

lose: perder

loss: perda

loud: alto(a)

low: baixo(a)

M

made-up: inventado(a)

major: importante, principal

matter: importar

measure: medida; medir

millennial: pessoa nascida nas decádas de 1980, 1990 e início dos anos 2000

misinterpret: interpretar mal

mislead: enganar

misrepresent: deturpar, desvirtuar

move out: mudar-se

N

need: necessidade

network: rede

newsroom: sala de imprensa

O

once: uma vez

ongoing: contínuo

other: outro

otherwise: de outro modo

outcome: resultado

outrage: indignação

outspoken: sincero(a), franco(a)

outstanding: excepcional, extraordinário

outwardly: exteriormente

own: possuir; próprio(a)

P

padding: enchimento

paint: tinta

pen pal: correspondente

pesky: chato, desagradável

pitch: jogar

pity: pena, piedade

plenty of: muito

portray: retratar

poverty: pobreza

powerful: poderoso(a)

privacy: privacidade

profit: lucro

proud: orgulhoso(a)

purpose: propósito, objetivo

R

raise: criar, educar; aumentar

random: aleatório(a)

range: gama, faixa, variedade

rate: taxa

recover: recuperar(-se)

regardless of: independentemente de, apesar de

reliable: confiável

relieved: aliviado(a)

rely: confiar

remain: permanecer

replace: substituir

require: requerer

research: pesquisa

retailer: revendedor

rewarding: gratificante

rise: aumento

room: espaço; quarto

S

sadness: tristeza

safe: seguro(a)

safe and sound: são e salvo/sã e salva

safety: segurança

satire: sátira

savvy: esclarecido(a), esperto(a)

scared: amedrontado(a), assustado(a)

scarf: cachecol

scratchy: arranhado(a)

scrawny: esquelético(a)

scroll: rolar

scrollbar: barra de rolagem

season: temporada

self-esteem: autoestima

self-harm: autoflagelar-se

settlement: assentamento, povoado

shape: forma, formato; formar, moldar

share: compartilhar; compartilhamento

shelter: abrigo

shift: mudança; mudar

shut out: excluir

sideways: de lado

sign: sinal, placa

silk: seda

since: desde

size: tamanho

slice: pedaço

slowly: devagar, vagarosamente

sneak out: esgueirar-se, sair sorrateiramente

soon: cedo

sort: tipo

spark: provocar, despertar

speech: fala

speech bubble: balão de fala

speed: velocidade

spend: passar, usar, gastar

spin: girar

spot: reconhecer, identificar

spread: espalhar

stable: estável

standstill: paralisação, inatividade

step-by-step: passo a passo

stranger: desconhecido

struggle: lutar

stuff: coisa(s)

suck: sugar

suddenly: de repente

suitable: adequado(a)

T

tailor: personalizar, ajustar

take over: assumir

target: alvo

target audience: público-alvo

thought: pensamento

thoughtful: cuidadoso(a), atencioso(a)

thread: linha

thrive: prosperar, crescer

throw up: vomitar

tie: amarrar

together: junto

toward: em direção a

treaty: tratado

trend: tendência

troll: pessoa que publica mensagens irritantes na internet a fim de obter atenção ou causar problema

trust: confiar

trusted: confiável, de confiança

twice: duas vezes

U

unchanging: imutável

unfortunately: infelizmente

unreliable: não confiável

unsafe: inseguro(a)

unsuitable: inadequado

untapped: inexplorado(a)

unwittingly: involuntariamente, inconscientemente

update: atualizar

upset: irritar, aborrecer; irritado(a), aborrecido(a)

useless: inútil

V

value: valorizar

W

warning: advertência, aviso

warning sign: placa de aviso

way: caminho; direção

weaponized: armamentizado(a), transformado(a) em arma

weigh: pesar

weight: peso

wellbeing: bem-estar

wide: amplo(a)

widely: amplamente

wireless: sem fio

wish: desejar; desejo

withdrawal: retirada

without: sem

workmate: colega de trabalho

worried: preocupado(a)

worry: preocupar-se

worse: pior

wrest: arrancar, obter

MY DIGITAL WORLD

It's time to decorate your tablet with stickers. Complete the tasks from the boxes **Challenge!/Extra Challenge!** to get stickers and customize your tablet.

12:00   4G   80%

- SETTINGS
- EMAIL
- STORE
- ENGLISH PLAY

	1st Challenge!	Extra Challenge!	2nd Challenge!	Extra Challenge!
UNIT 1	✓ ✗	✓ ✗	✓ ✗	✓ ✗
UNIT 2	✓ ✗	✓ ✗	✓ ✗	✓ ✗
UNIT 3	✓ ✗	✓ ✗	✓ ✗	✓ ✗
UNIT 4	✓ ✗	✓ ✗	✓ ✗	✓ ✗
UNIT 5	✓ ✗	✓ ✗	✓ ✗	✓ ✗
UNIT 6	✓ ✗	✓ ✗	✓ ✗	✓ ✗
UNIT 7	✓ ✗	✓ ✗	✓ ✗	✓ ✗
UNIT 8	✓ ✗	✓ ✗	✓ ✗	✓ ✗

Stickers

Conheça seu livro Page 7	🥇		🥈	🥉
Test (Units 1 and 2) Page 39	🥇		🥈	🥉
Test (Units 3 and 4) Page 65	🥇		🥈	🥉
Test (Units 5 and 6) Page 91	🥇		🥈	🥉
Test (Units 7 and 8) Page 117	🥇		🥈	🥉
Play 'n' Learn 1 Page 39	☹️	🙄	🙂	😀
Play 'n' Learn 2 Page 65	☹️	🙄	🙂	😀
Play 'n' Learn 3 Page 91	☹️	🙄	🙂	😀
Play 'n' Learn 4 Page 117	☹️	🙄	🙂	😀

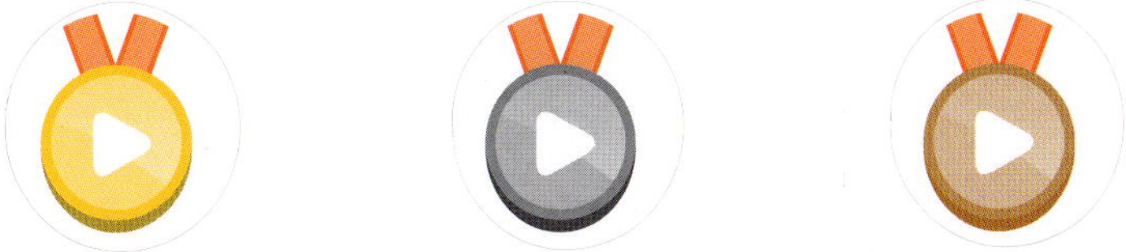

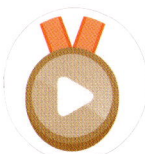

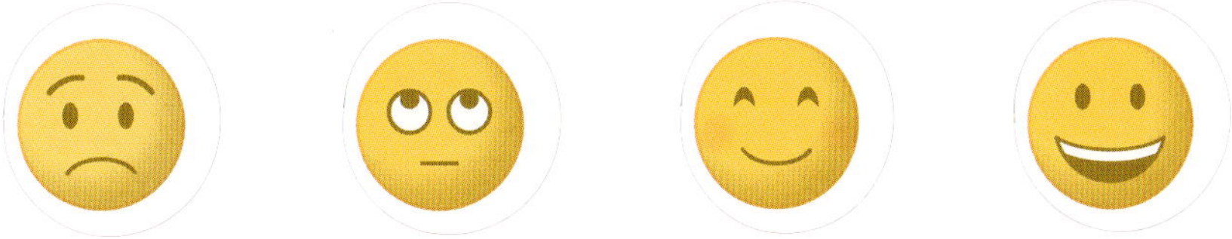

Stickers 147

Play 'n' Learn 1
Page 39

a video player app   a contacts app   an instant messenger app

Play 'n' Learn 2
Page 65

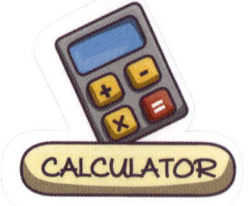

a clock app   a calculator app   a camera app

Play 'n' Learn 3
Page 91

an e-reader app   a browser app   a music player app

Play 'n' Learn 4
Page 117

a weather app   a maps app   a calendar app

Glossary

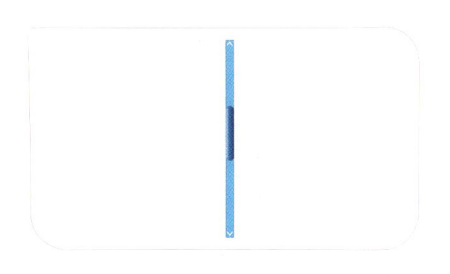

Stickers 151

Glossary

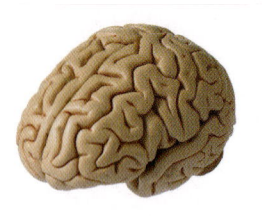

Stickers 155

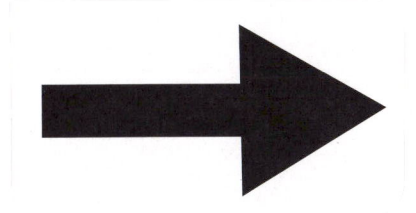